By Sue Harper and S. Lesley Buxton

TIME TO WONDER

A Kid's Guide to BC's Regional Museums

VOLUME 2: VANCOUVER ISLAND, SALT SPRING, ALERT BAY, AND HAIDA GWAII

RMB

TABLE OF CONTENTS

LAND ACKNOWLEDGEMENTS

We would like to acknowledge that when we visit, work or research in the museums and centres in this book we are working and exploring on the traditional and unceded territories of the following First Nations People:

T'Sou-ke and Pacheedaht (SOOKE REGION MUSEUM AND VISITOR CENTRE)

Lekwungen, Esquimalt and Songhees (CRAIGDARROCH CASTLE)

Lekwungen, Esquimalt, Songhees, Swengwhung Family Group (POINT ELLICE HOUSE MUSEUM AND GARDENS)

ləkʷəŋən, Songhees, Esquimalt and W̱SÁNEĆ (CITY OF VICTORIA)

Lekwungen, Esquimalt and Songhees (THE MARITIME MUSEUM OF BRITISH COLUMBIA)

Quw'utsun (Cowichan) (BC FOREST DISCOVERY CENTRE)

Hupačasath, Tseshaht (ALBERNI VALLEY MUSEUM)

Yuułuʔiłʔatḥ (UCLUELET AQUARIUM)

Qualicum (QUALICUM BEACH MUSEUM)

K'ómoks (CUMBERLAND MUSEUM AND ARCHIVES)

We Wai Kai, Wei Wai Kum, Kwiakah, Awahoo, Nuyumbalees (MUSEUM AT CAMPBELL RIVER)

Saanich, Quw'utsun (Cowichan) and Chemainus (SALT SPRING MUSEUM)

'Namgis (U'MISTA CULTURAL CENTRE, THE WHALE INTERPRETIVE CENTRE)

Haida (SAAHLINDA NAAY – SAVING THINGS HOUSE)

We recognize that these many Indigenous Peoples have thousands of years of culture and history on this land, culture and history we value and hope to learn from.

WHOSE VOICES ARE WE HEARING?

Next time you go to a museum we want you to do us a favour. We want you to imagine at closing time you get locked in – yes, you heard us – we said locked in, and, yes, by yourself, kind of like the movie *Night at the Museum*.

We know what you're thinking. You're thinking these writers are crazy, and you're probably right, but please bear with us.

Now imagine while you're standing there alone in the museum that everything suddenly comes alive and is able to speak. After you've stopped screaming, what do you think you'll notice first?

Maybe you'll notice the beautiful jade adze you admired earlier. It speaks in the ancient language of the Indigenous master carver who used it.

The watercolour painting, just by the gift shop, has the sing-song voice of the young girl who painted it many, many years ago.

The boat you saw in the main gallery only speaks a few words in English, like the mother who supported her family by delivering her fresh vegetables to the big city, and who always gave back to her new community.

The baseball jersey has the laugh of the boy who once scored home runs in it.

Imagine what you'd hear? How many different voices? How many attitudes and opinions? Can you imagine all the characters and their secrets?

Museums are alive with the voices and perspectives of the people whose belongings are in them. Listen carefully and you can hear all sorts of stories from Canada's Indigenous Peoples, settlers and new Canadians, as well as people from all over the world. Not all these stories are happy; some of them are heartbreaking, others will just make you angry, and that's OK. Anger is a powerful motivator. Sometimes the only time things get changed is when people get angry.

History can be inspirational and can offer us strength when we feel lost. It can also flood us with a mishmash of feelings that contradict each other.

At times it can even make us proud.

Nowadays museums are working hard to make sure everyone in our community is heard. Not just because it's important to share – hey, we all learned that in kindergarten, right? But because we all know how it feels to be ignored. Nobody likes it. It's like putting up your hand in class and never getting called on, even though you have a lot to say.

We know there are a lot of words in this book in languages you might never have heard before, but don't be afraid of them. Give it a go and try to say them. These languages are important. We have to work hard to make sure they don't disappear.

Listening to only one voice is like eating a bowl of oatmeal for breakfast every day. Nice for maybe a day or two, but forever? Boring! Perspectives, like the best breakfasts, are filled with different flavours. It's variety that makes our community so wonderful.

So the next time you enter a museum, remember to listen. You never know what you might hear.

SOUTHERN VANCOUVER ISLAND

Duncan – BC Forest
Discovery Centre

Sooke
Region
Museum

Point Ellice House
Museum and Garde

Maritime Museum
of British Columbia

The Craigdarrock
Castle

VICTORIA & SURROUNDS

VANCOUVER ISLAND

THE SOUTH, VICTORIA & SURROUNDS

The South, Victoria & Surrounds

1 SOOKE REGION MUSEUM

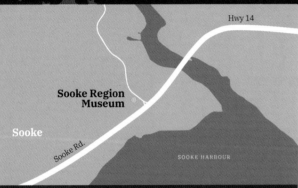

Hwy 14

Sooke Region Museum

Sooke

Sooke Rd.

SOOKE HARBOUR

JUST THE FACTS

WHERE IS IT? 2070 Phillips Road, Sooke, BC, V9Z 0Y3; Toll Free 1-866-888-4748
sookeregionmuseum.com

ARE PHOTOGRAPHS ALLOWED? Yes, but no flash.

HOW DID IT START? The creation of this museum was a true community effort. In 1974 the Sooke Lions Club volunteered to take on the responsibility of building the museum. The Sooke Community Association donated the property where the museum now stands. A government grant helped with some of the costs, in addition to donations from the local business community. An army of volunteer workers from the Lions Club and the community helped with the construction. This museum would never have become a reality if not for the support of many.

WHERE HAS IT LIVED?

Since June 11, 1977, when the museum opened its doors for its first function, a BBQ and dance to celebrate its completion, the museum has lived in the same place. The Sooke Region Historical Society, which was formed in 1974, runs the museum. Sooke is known as the "Volunteer Capital of Canada."

WHERE DO THE ITEMS COME FROM?

Items are donated to the museum. In fact, as soon as the community got word that the proposed museum was being built, things began to pour in. Early donations were photographs and farm equipment.

HOW HAS IT CHANGED?

The museum is a dynamic space, and constantly evolving. The museum's photo collection can now be viewed online. A new forestry Trail and Outdoor exhibit featuring the museum's steam donkey is being developed, as well as an online exhibit about the role of women in Sooke. In addition to this, staff and volunteers are always busy overhauling and working on existing exhibits.

Learn how light works

TRIANGLE ISLAND LIGHTHOUSE

he Triangle Island Lighthouse, stablished in 1910, sat pproximately 50 kilometres orthwest of Cape Scott on he northern extremity of ancouver Island on a plateau n the island. It was built to help ith the navigation of ships.

Both labourers and materials for the lighthouse arrived on the SS *Leebro*.

ruel winds damaged the ghthouse tower, duplex welling and wireless shack as oon as they were built.

It took about ten years for the lighthouse keepers and radio operators to acknowledge that the lighthouse was completely hostile to the humans who operated the station.

The island is so steep that a tramway was built to take supplies up to the plateau where the dwellings were built.

nside the lighthouse is the stevan Point First Order resnel lens. It's not the riginal lens, but these lenses, hich are **first-order lenses**, e so rare it's important to **reserve** them.

Because of the large size of the lens, it came in pieces to the museum, like a jigsaw puzzle, and had to be re-assembled.

Today the concrete base of the lighthouse remains on the island.

The island is also known as the Anne Vallée Ecological Reserve, after a biologist who died while researching the island's tufted puffins. No one is allowed on the island unless they have a permit, and there must be at least two people.

Every lighthouse has its own lamp flash pattern (Triangle Island's is four flashes every ten seconds) and **unique** foghorn sound.

The lens works the same way as a grandfather clock, using hand-cranked weights that rotate the lens as they descend.

COUGAR

JUST THE FACTS

WHAT IS IT? A mounted male cougar preserved through **taxidermy**. Sooke is a popular hangout for cougars. It's estimated 600–800 cougars live on Vancouver Island.

WHAT DOES IT LOOK LIKE? He looks like a giant version of your cat, only fiercer and heavier. Males weigh around 60 kilograms; that's about the weight of two adult Labrador dogs. This one has a ferocious gaze, and his muscular body is ready to spring into action. Most of his body is covered in yellowish-brown fur, except for under his chin and on his neck where his fur is white.

WHERE DOES IT COME FROM? He was shot by a Sooke man, George Pedneault, who started tracking cougars when he was 13 and kept a pack of cougar hounds on call for emergencies.

WHO USED IT? The cougar has been in the museum's natural history section since it arrived. It's on permanent loan to the museum from George Pedneault.

Tell Me More

The museum has another cougar **pelt** in its collection. This one is kept in storage. It was shot in the 1940s by the "Cougar Lady," Joan Milwarde-Yates. A photo of this woman can be seen in the museum. A lifelong Metchosin resident, the Cougar Lady was known by all as a crack shot. Metchosin is about 15 minutes from Sooke. Back then, farmers there kept animals such as dairy and beef cattle, pigs, sheep, chickens and turkeys – basically dinner for cougars. If there was a problem with a cougar, they'd go to the Cougar Lady for help. Word is that she was very good at her job. Many families lived on the bounties they received for cougar pelts. It was part of how they survived. In the 1940s the government rate for a pelt was 15 dollars.

? WOULD YOU BELIEVE?

The play Cougar Annie Tales *by Kat Kadoski tells the story of Annie (Ada Annie Jordan), nicknamed Cougar Annie, who lived in Boat Basin, a remote area of Vancouver Island, where she kept a small mail order nursery business. She earned her nickname for defending it, and her family, from over 60 cougars.*

Cougar Annie's House in 1998
Photo: Paper ripper 1968, Wikipedia

⭐ WHY IS THE COUGAR IMPORTANT IN THIS AREA?

This piece of taxidermy shows what a cougar looks like. Though cougars are part of our community, many people may not know what they look like, or how big they are. It represents our need to learn how to coexist with our animal neighbours. In Sooke, an organization called Wild Wise works hard to educate people. On its Facebook page, it posts stories about cougar sightings, **conservation** and wildlife **rehabilitation** centres. It's important that we learn how to avoid conflict with wild creatures by doing simple things like changing the way we get rid of our garbage and cleaning our BBQs after use. In BC, the Conservation Officer Service gets about 2,500 calls a year about cougars. Usually these turn out to be something else; contact is very rare with these shy creatures.

My Turn

What wild animals live in your neighbourhood? Do some research and find out how you can coexist more easily with them.

CONNECTIONS

The ancient Egyptians kept all sorts of exotic animals like baboons, monkeys, gazelles, falcons, lions, mongooses and even hippos. Dogs and cats were still just as popular as they are today. They began to preserve deceased animals around 2200 BC. The pets of high-ranking people were preserved with spices and oils in order that they could be buried with their owners. In order to ensure they'd meet again with their beloved pet after death in the **Field of Reeds**.

These are animal Mummies on display at the Royal Ontario Museum
Wikimedia Commons: Daderot

JUST THE FACTS

WHAT IS IT? Trophies from the annual All Sooke Day, the longest-running annual logger sports event in the Western world. It ran from 1934 until 2002. The event began during the **Great Depression** as a community effort to cheer people up. "It was a celebration of the progress of Sooke."

WHAT DOES IT LOOK LIKE? A collection of mounted, silver-plated trophies with **inscriptions** and dates. Some of the trophies are scuffed and chipped, while others have parts missing. The trophy for Canadian Championship **Peavey Log Roller** features a gold-coloured figurine of a man with an axe mounted on a gold-coloured pole.

WHERE DOES IT COME FROM? Most of the trophies were privately donated.

WHO USED IT? These cups were awarded for competitions for best baby, horseshoe pitching, tree chopping, bucking, axe throwing, tug-of-war, egg rolling, tree climbing and **log birling.**

Tell Me More

One of the annual highlights was the famous spring salmon barbeque, cooked in the traditional Indigenous way: split open, flattened and cooked on a rack that is stood up like a triangle, with alderwood coals in between. Beef was served as well. This was cooked in the method of the **Leechtown miners**, wrapped in a **gunny sack** and soaked in Sooke River water for 12 hours, then buried under coals in a firepit and cooked overnight. Leechtown was a gold-mining town about 20 kilometres north of Sooke. Today it is a ghost town.

TROPHIES FROM ALL SOOKE DAY

WOULD YOU BELIEVE?

The peavey log roll event was created in, and unique to, Sooke. Peaveys are poles with a hinged, spiked hook on the end and are used by loggers to roll logs. A peavey is sometimes called a log wrench.

Images:
Pearson Scott Foresman
via Wikipedia

CONNECTIONS

In Quebec they celebrate another community festival: the Québec Winter Carnival. This marvellous event features Bonhomme, a 2.2-metre-tall magical creature made out of 182 kilograms of snow. A stylish fellow, Bonhomme is famous for wearing a red toque and an arrow sash – a traditional woven piece worn around the waist, popular with French Canadians beginning around the 1770s. The festival began in 1894 as a way to escape the gloom of the cold Quebec winter. At the first festival there was an ice palace, ice sculptures, a masquerade on ice, a canoe race across the frozen St. Lawrence River and parade floats. Sadly, the festival came to an end during the Depression and did not restart until 1955, when the city's mayor gave Bonhomme the keys to the city. Since then, people from across the globe have come to love this yearly event and its mascot.

My Turn

Host your own egg and spoon race. All you need is a spoon for each contestant, a boiled egg and a racetrack. The person who makes it all the way around without racking their egg is the winner.

WHY IS ALL SOOKE DAY IMPORTANT IN THIS AREA?

The festival was started to raise community spirit after the Great Depression. It was a way to celebrate their good fortune in having a local **economy** supported by logging and fishing. The First Annual Celebration of the Progress of Sooke took place on Wednesday, July 25, 1934, at the Sooke River Flats. Later it was renamed "All Sooke Day." It ran for almost 70 years before it came to its end in 2002.

Originally, it took place on a Wednesday when department stores in Victoria closed at noon. Visitors from Victoria arrived by the busload. The day featured events like the tombola (raffle), gold-panning demonstrations, egg and spoon races (sometimes the eggs weren't even boiled!), a pie-eating contest and best baby. The logging events were the most popular, as they highlighted the skill of experienced loggers. Over the years these became so popular the festival attracted entrants from all over the world.

2 CRAIGDARROCH CASTLE

Photo: The Craigdarroch Castle Historical Museum Society

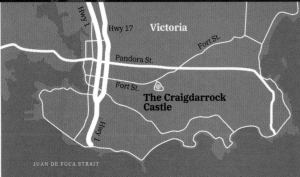

JUST THE FACTS

WHERE IS IT? 1050 Joan Crescent, Victoria, BC, V8S 3L5; (250) 592-5323

thecastle.ca

ARE PHOTOGRAPHS ALLOWED? Yes.

HOW DID IT START? This museum began its life as a "bonanza castle." This is what people used to call the huge mansions owned by the rich. It was built for the coal baron Robert Dunsmuir and his family in an architectural style inspired by Scottish castles. Robert didn't start life as a millionaire. When he immigrated to Canada from Scotland, he worked as a miner. By the time he died, he was the richest man in British Columbia.

WHERE HAS IT LIVED?

The museum has always been in the same place. But over the years many different people have walked its halls. Sadly, Robert Dunsmuir was not one of them. He died before the castle was finished. On its completion, his wife, Joan, and their three unmarried daughters and two orphaned grandchildren lived there. Imagine six people living in a house the size of an apartment building. When Joan died, her daughters sold her home to a real estate developer, who divided the land and raffled off the castle. The winners of the castle eventually lost it to the bank when the bills piled up. Next the castle became home to a military hospital caring for soldiers who'd served in the Great War. Then it became Victoria College. Visitors can still see the students' graffiti scrawled on the walls. After the college outgrew the castle, the Victoria School Board moved in.

WHERE DO THE ITEMS COME FROM?

Some of the items belonged to the Dunsmuirs, other items were donated and some were bought especially for the museum.

HOW HAS IT CHANGED?

Luckily, in 1959, James K. Nesbitt, the Castle Society's founding president, set up a Heritage Society to preserve the castle. But it wasn't until ten years later that it was able to move in. Even then, it only had part of the house. It had to share it with the Victoria Conservatory of Music. The music school was a busy place, with 30 pianos and lots of young students. Eventually, the music school moved out and the society finally took over the building. Since then, the society has worked hard to restore the castle. Thanks to its hard work, it's now a National Historic Site famed throughout Canada.

feel what it was like to live in a castle

LATE 19TH-CENTURY BLACK FOREST MANTLE CLOCK

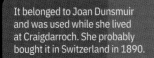

It belonged to Joan Dunsmuir and was used while she lived at Craigdarroch. She probably bought it in Switzerland in 1890.

Japy's assembly line system was so successful he used it to make other items like coffee grinders, **enamelware** and kitchen utensils.

The clock is decorated with a carved wildlife scene featuring a family of red deer. These animals were super popular during the Victorian period. They were used to decorate lots of household items. Even today this happens with some creatures. Remember the recent craze for unicorns?

The clock is by the French company, Japy Frères & Co. The founder of this company, Frédéric Japy, completely changed the way clocks were made. He built a manufacturing plant in his hometown of Beaucourt, France, and created an assembly line system so that the clocks were quickly made on a schedule.

Even though this is called a Black Forest carving, and named after a forest in Germany, it was made in a workshop in Brienz, Switzerland.

Wealthy tourists on a **grand tour** often bought pieces by master carvers. For those travelling on a budget, there were still plenty of choices. Favourites included cuckoo clocks, tea caddies and coat hooks.

In 1884 the School of Woodcarving in Brienz was founded. The school kept a collection of real and stuffed animals for the students to observe up close.

Brienz is home to a street called Brunngasse, once awarded the title of most beautiful street in Europe. It has cobblestones and is filled with 18th-century wooden chalets that look like they belong on a cuckoo clock.

JUST THE FACTS

WHAT IS IT? A **papier mâché** toy French bulldog from the late 19th century made in France. The toy was available in a variety of breeds: English bulldog, French bulldog, Boston terrier and French snapping bulldog.

WHAT DOES IT LOOK LIKE? A **caricature** of a French bulldog. Nicknamed the "Growler" and the "Nodder," the dog barks and its head nods when it's pulled. Some people think this toy might be an early version of a bobblehead doll. The dog is ankle height and has castors under its feet, which make it moveable so it can be taken on a walk. It's a perfect pet with its bulging glass eyes, sculpted body and a white and reddish-brown coat. Originally, it wore a straw collar, but now it wears a black ribbon.

WHERE DOES IT COME FROM? It was bought from a collector/dealer.

WHO USED IT? Joan Dunsmuir's great-grandson Dermot de Trafford played with the toy dog.

TOY FRENCH BULLDOG

Collectors of antique toys love Growlers, especially in good condition. Even damaged, they can cost as much as $900. A Growler in good condition might be worth as much as $5,000. Not bad for a toy dog.

My Turn

Is there a dog in your life? A family pet, or one you just like? Why not do some research on the history of its breed. (If it's a mutt, you'll have to do a little more research.) You'll be surprised by what you find out. For example, did you know French bulldogs originated in Britain?

CONNECTIONS

Did you know there was a French bulldog on the RMS *Titanic* when it sank in the North Atlantic Ocean on April 15, 1912, after striking an iceberg? His name was Gamin de Pycombe. He was 2 years old. French bulldogs are terrible swimmers because of their strange proportions – a big head and short legs. His owner was a 27-year-old banker named Robert Daniel, who paid about £150 for him. Nowadays that's almost the price of a small, cheap car. Mr. Daniel survived the disaster and later claimed insurance for the drowned dog.

Tell Me More

French bulldogs were considered very fashionable during this time period. Images of them decorated everything from **inkwells** to cuckoo clocks. In Europe royalty loved them. In American society these dogs were owned by the wealthiest of families like the Rockefellers. Today these dogs are still very trendy. The star of Disney's *Moana*, Dwayne Johnson (**aka** "the Rock") has one called Hobbs. He often posts photos of them together at the gym. Popstar Lady Gaga has four Frenchies. One of them, a female called Asia, is a popular Instagram celebrity.

Gamin de Pycombe, the French Bulldog from The Titanic with owner Mr. Daniel.

★ WHY IS THE TOY FRENCH BULLDOG IMPORTANT IN THIS AREA?

It's not often one gets a chance to see a rare toy like the Growler. They were delicate and vulnerable to damage due to their papier mâché construction. Not many of them survived the demands of time, and in fact some were even crushed by the family dog.

TOY SOLDIER

JUST THE FACTS

WHAT IS IT? A CBG Mignot Company toy soldier wearing the uniform of a French military trooper.

WHAT DOES IT LOOK LIKE? This handsome moustached fellow wears a navy blue jacket over a white tunic with gold buttons, white pants with thin red and blue stripes and an elegant black hat with a red feather. On his back he wears a brown backpack. In his hands he holds a **musket** and a bent **bayonet**.

WHERE DOES IT COME FROM? his soldier is part of a set that included 11 troopers, one officer, one **standard bearer** and one drummer. The set came from a very famous toyshop in New York City called F.A.O. Schwarz Ltd. This store has been around for a 150 years. The set was bought at Schwarz's by the donor.

WHO USED IT? We don't know.

Tell Me More

C.B.G. Mignot Company is a French company that has been making toy soldiers since 1825, almost 200 years. Still today each figure is **cast**, assembled and painted by hand just like when the company began. This takes a long time, but it assures quality. The castle's soldier was made in the same way. The head was cast separately and attached to the body, which is solid lead. The musket is tin, a soft metal, which might explain why it's bent. The soldier is 5.6 x 2 cm in size – about the same as a clothes peg.

Photo: The Craigdarroch Castle Historical Museum Society. 992.011.011

14

You can visit C.B.G. Mignot in Anjou, France. The first floor of its workshop houses an exhibition room filled with its creations. On your way out, depending on the day of the week, you might pass by its figurine painter and welder.

CONNECTIONS

Only wealthy kids could afford toys soldiers until a toymaker named William Britain Jr. invented hollow cast leads, which means the soldiers were hollow, unlike the soldier at the castle. This technology revolutionized the industry and introduced an affordable line. The soldiers were made to scale and featured armies from England, the United States, France and Germany. There were many famous collectors, including Winston Churchill, who was the British prime minster during the Second World War.

⭐ WHY IS THE TOY SOLDIER IMPORTANT IN THIS AREA?

The soldier ties us to the past and reminds us that even a hundred years ago kids were playing with similar toys. The only difference is how our toys are made. Nowadays we know that lead can be very dangerous for children. In Canada it's banned from toys.

My Turn

Take a moment to think about your favourite toy. Do you think kids will be playing with something similar in a hundred years?

Children have enjoyed their toys since before history was even written

Top left: Little horse on wheels (Ancient greek child's Toy). Sharon Mollerus, Flickr

Top right: Construction toys have been popular since the 20th century. These are Lego™ bricks. photo: Alan Chia, Wikipedia.

Middle left: The doll of Crepereia Tryphaena, from Rome, second century AD. Umknown author. Wikipedia

Middle centre: European bisque doll from the 1870s. Photo: Andreas Praefcke. Wikipedia

Middle right: A boy with a hoop. Hoops have long been a popular toy across a variety of cultures. Circa 1902. Author unknown

Bottom: Set of 40 cast metal World War I era toy soldiers,, ca. 1925. Photo: Flickr, Catfisheye

JUST THE FACTS

REPRODUCTION OF AN 1890S STAINED GLASS WINDOW

WHAT IS IT? A reproduction of a stained glass window that decorates Craigdarroch Castle's drawing room. The original was crafted by the Pacific Art Glass Company of San Francisco. The reproduction was made by Robert McCausland Limited of Toronto.

WHAT DOES IT LOOK LIKE? The window is based on a painting called *Odalisque* by Sir Frederic Leighton. It features a woman leaning against a wall, wearing a blouse and long skirt, holding a peacock feather fan. A swan looks up at her as if they are talking to each other. In the distance there's a view of a nearby mosque. This could have been inspired by Leda and the Swan, a Greek myth.

WHERE DOES IT COME FROM? In 1999 the Castle Society used a donated black-and-white photograph to recreate this piece. The photograph was taken in 1928 at the donor's wedding.

WHO USED IT? Over the years many people have stood in front of this window admiring its beauty.

Tell Me More

The original window was broken during a snowball fight. The culprits were Victoria College students. Victor Rogers, one of the students who witnessed it, said a snowball hit the woman's face and smashed it. Not long afterwards he said the window was removed. It was stored in the Castle's boiler room. Victor never saw it again.

The donor of the photograph thought putting the window in the boiler room would keep it safe, but while it was there, it was damaged further.

My Turn

Learn how to make your own super cool tissue paper stained glass hearts. You might need some help from an adult as there's cooking involved.
Visit https://www.youtube.com/watch?v=X9Udx9xf4rY.

CONNECTIONS

Smoking rooms were very popular when the castle was built. Even Queen Victoria had one in her seaside home on the Isle of Wight. This was a place where, after dinner, men would gather to smoke cigars. It was considered **scandalous** for women to smoke.

WHY IS THE STAINED GLASS WINDOW IMPORTANT IN THIS AREA?

The castle has one of the most impressive Victorian residential stained and leaded glass window collections in North America. Thirty-two of the 47 original art glass windows are still in place. The majority of the pieces feature flower themes, except for the piece inspired by Leighton's *Odalisque* and another in the smoking room believed to be either Robert Dunsmuir, or the Elizabethan explorer Sir Walter Raleigh. Take a look for yourself on the castle's website. Compare the photographs of the coal baron with the image on the stained glass. Who do you think the window looks like?

The earliest depiction of a European man smoking, from *Tobacco* by Anthony Chute, 1595.
Source: Wikipedia

JUST THE FACTS

SILVER EARWAX SPOON

WHAT IS IT? A silver earwax spoon that was part of a fancy sewing kit in a heart-shaped red box. The kit included a needle, a thimble and a small pair of scissors.

WHAT DOES IT LOOK LIKE? It looks like a spoon for feeding baby birds or a pet gerbil. The bowl of the spoon is tiny. The long handle of the spoon widens into a pair of tweezers.

WHERE DOES IT COME FROM? A collector of antique needlework items donated it to the castle.

WHO USED IT? We don't know exactly who used this item. Kits like these were common while the Dunsmuir family lived in the castle. It might seem odd to us, but earwax spoons were a regular part of sewing kits during the 18th and 19th centuries.

Tell Me More

The earwax spoon was included in the kit because before waxed thread was available seamstresses often used their earwax to strengthen their thread. Earwax, also known as cerumen, is a sticky mixture of dead cells and natural **secretions** that help to protect the ear canal.

Earwax can also prevent threads from fraying, strengthen them and improve the ability of the thread to glide through layers of fabric. Another sewing tool used with earwax was the bodkin. It was a sharp tool used to make holes in cloth and leather. Some bodkins had an ear scoop on the other end. This made it easier to gather wax and apply it to the thread.

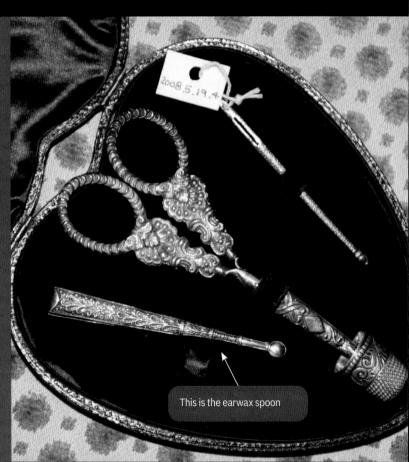

This is the earwax spoon

Photo: The Craigdarroch Castle Historical Museum Society. 2008.005.019.003

WOULD YOU BELIEVE?

Throughout history people have believed earwax has **medicinal** *qualities. Pliny the Elder, a famous Roman writer, recommended it for treating scorpion stings and snakebites. Oswald Croll, a German* **alchemist** *and professor of medicine in the 1500s, recommended earwax as a way to treat wounds. What would you think if your caregiver tried to smear your cuts with earwax?*

My Turn

Make your own paints – no, not with earwax! With flour:

- Combine ½ cup flour, ½ cup salt, ½ cup water and mix until smooth.
- Divide mixture into three recycled yogurt containers and add a few drops of food colour to each.
- Mix again, add more water for thinner paint.
- Pour into a squeezable container like an icing sugar bag.

Voila, you have paint!

Over the years people have used earwax to do some crazy stuff. In medieval times the monks working on **illuminated manuscripts** – think of these as the most beautiful books you've ever seen filled with gorgeous illustrations, decorative borders and even real gold – used earwax, sugar, eggs and urine to prepare and **bind pigments**.

WHY IS THE SILVER EARWAX SPOON IMPORTANT IN THIS AREA?

We know all different types and classes of women would've used earwax spoons. Still, whatever a woman's **status** was, an earwax spoon was a well-used tool. Some women would have used it while sewing decorative lace on their collars and cuffs. Other women would have used it while sewing and repairing for their employers or families. The earwax spoon was used for all kinds of needlework.

Photo by Vlada Karpovich from Pexels

JUST THE FACTS

HAND-CARVED MINIATURE BED

WHAT IS IT? A tiny bed about the size of a cellphone that belongs to a collection of **rococo**-style, hand-carved, dollhouse furniture.

WHAT DOES IT LOOK LIKE? This fancy miniature bed features a hand-carved bed frame complete with carved head – and footboards. The carvings look like climbing vines. Each corner of the bed has **milled finials**. The mattress is missing, but there are slats to support one. The bed's feet are thick at the top and thin at the bottom. It looks like the kind of bed a princess like Sleeping Beauty would use.

WHERE DOES IT COME FROM? In 1960 Jean, Elizabeth and Catherine Macdonald donated it to the museum.

WHO USED IT? The great-granddaughters of Robert and Joan Dunsmuir, Jean, Elizabeth and Catherine Macdonald. Known as "the Macdonald sisters," these lucky girls lived a privileged life in upper-class Victoria society. They played with this toy at their home Duntulm, a farm in North Saanich.

Photo: The Craigdarroch Castle Historical Museum Society. 983.314.001

WOULD YOU BELIEVE?

Adults used to play with dollhouses. The trend began in Northern Europe in the 17th century as an adult amusement that allowed them to show off their wealth and their standing in the community. In Holland they were called cabinet houses and had hinges allowing them to open or close depending on who was visiting. In Germany they were called dockenhaus, *meaning miniature house.*

CONNECTIONS

The oldest collection of toys in the world was found in a child's grave in Siberia, Russia. These finds are 4,500 years old – that's about 40 great-grandpas ago. The toys belonged to a child who lived in an **Okunev** community during the **Bronze Age**. The discovery included an ancient doll carved out of **soapstone** with expressive facial features. It's believed the doll belonged to an ordinary kid, rather than one who came from a wealthy family. **Archeologists** have found other ancient dolls. Dolls called paddle dolls made out of wood, with roughly made bodies and long hair, have been found in Egyptian tombs. Clay dolls have been found from ancient Greece. It seems that kids no matter where or when they are from have always enjoyed pretending.

It doesn't really look like much to us, but this is a typical Egyptian paddle doll from 2080–1990 BC.

Jason210. English Wikipedia

My Turn

Learn how to make a miniature bunk bed using a shoebox with Mary Miniaturas DIY (https://www.youtube.com/watch?v=FNlH-hF8-jY). You might need an adult to help with some of the cutting and sewing, but the rest looks pretty easy.

Tell Me More

Most likely the furniture set came to the sisters through their mother's side. Though there are no photos of the girls playing with the set, the museum does have a framed photograph of the three sisters in raincoats and hats lying on a blanket spread out on a lawn of the castle. The girls are all facing the camera and smiling as if they are having fun.

⭐ WHY IS THE HAND-CARVED MINIATURE BED IMPORTANT IN THIS AREA?

The toy tells us about the kind of lives the younger members of the Dunsmuir family led. How they played, and what they enjoyed playing with. At the same time, it's important to remember these children led very privileged lives. This means they had special advantages because they came from a wealthy family that was believed to be important. Most parents during this time didn't have the kind of money they could spend on toys like these.

3 POINT ELLICE HOUSE MUSEUM AND GARDENS

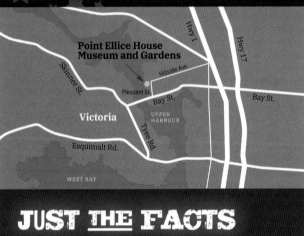

Point Ellice House Museum and Gardens

JUST THE FACTS

WHERE IS IT? 2616 Pleasant Street, Victoria, BC, V8T 4V3; (250) 380-6506
pointellicehouse.com

ARE PHOTOGRAPHS ALLOWED? Yes, but no flash.

HOW DID IT START? The O'Reillys knew their home, Point Ellice House, was special. They tried opening a museum, but it was too expensive. So they offered the province a choice: help with the costs of running a museum, or buy the house.

Not surprisingly, the province decided to buy the house. Built in an Italianate villa design, a style famous for its fancy arches and columns, the house had once been one of the grandest in Victoria.

WHERE HAS IT LIVED?

The house still stands exactly where it was built. Back in 1861, when Point Ellice House was built, it was located in one of the most fashionable areas in Victoria. Now the house and its garden are a small haven of green in the heart of a busy industrial district.

WHERE DO THE ITEMS COME FROM?

In 1975, when John and Inez O'Reilly sold their home, Point Ellice House, to the Province of British Columbia, they did something unusual. They left practically everything they owned in it – furniture, pots and pans, paintings and even letters. This was a big deal as the O'Reilly family had lived there for over a hundred years.

HOW HAS IT CHANGED?

There have been many repairs made to the historic house. Like any other old house, Point Ellice House requires ongoing maintenance. The old windows and floors were mended. An exhibition area with an interpretation centre was built to stage special local presentations, and the kitchen garden has been fully restored. The museum personnel are always learning more about the site. For instance, they recently uncovered a historic brick pathway they didn't even know was there.

The museum also brings stories to visitors that were previously ignored – particularly the story of the colonization of BC. Peter O'Reilly, John's grandfather, was an Indian reserve commissioner. His job was to decide how reserves were set out. Now the museum is working to tell the story of colonization so that we (non-Indigenous people) can think about how we might address colonialism's **injustices** now and in the future.

Imagine what life was like in the 1860s

ALBION FRENCH RANGE STOVE

The stove was bought at a local Victoria company, Albion Iron Works, in 1889 by Peter and Caroline O'Reilly. Peter recorded the event in his diary.

en this stove was bought, oria was the most populated in British Columbia.

Not only was this stove used to cook dinner but it was also connected to a water boiler so it heated water for the entire house.

877 the *Home Cook Book* was a ular Canadian cookbook. It was inted over and over. It's thought to he oldest **community cookbook** in ada. It was written to raise money he oldest children's hospital in ada – Sick Kids Hospital in Toronto, ch opened in 1875. The cookbook ded housekeeping advice and oters dedicated to table talk and **uette**. It also featured a delicious be for chocolate pudding that could erved with whipped cream. Yum.

Albion Iron Works also made rails for the Fraser Canyon, the most dangerous section of the Canadian Pacific Railway (CPR). Seven thousand men worked the Fraser Canyon section. The majority of them were Chinese. The Chinese workers were paid less than white workers. They got $1.00 a day and paid for their own equipment. White workers were paid $1.50–1.75 a day and were given equipment. The Chinese workers were given the riskiest jobs. It's thought that four Chinese workers died for every 1.6 kilometres of track laid.

Albion Iron Works made boat stoves. These were much smaller than Peter and Caroline O'Reilly's stove. These were used for heat, as well as cooking and baking.

o: Christeah Dupont, Assistant Curator.

JUST THE FACTS

MARY AUGUSTA'S PAINTING

WHAT IS IT? A watercolour painting on ruled paper created by Mary Augusta O'Reilly, the second daughter of Peter and Caroline O'Reilly. She made the painting when she was only 6. This talented young artist was often sick, so she was tutored at home. She was cared for by her grandmother, Charlotte Trutch. Two weeks before her seventh birthday she died. Her grandmother died the next day.

WHAT DOES IT LOOK LIKE? The painting is very skillful for such a young person. Mary Augusta has painted a cozy-looking red house that looks like Point Ellice, a pathway that winds through a garden and a green fence. There are mountains and a large fir tree in the background.

WHERE DOES IT COME FROM? It's part of the collection purchased by the museum from the O'Reillys' grandson John.

WHO USED IT? It probably belonged to Mary Augusta's mother and father. It was most likely a treasured keepsake and reminder of their child.

Image: Point Ellice House: PEH1975.001.922

My Turn

Try making a painting of your home. What do you think people in the future would discover about you looking at your painting? What do you think will stay the same about houses in the future, and what do you think will be different?

Tell Me More

The watercolour painting was made on lined paper that was torn out of an exercise book. Mary Augusta signed it as if it's finished, but is it possible she got tired and gave up on the painting? The mountains in the background don't look completed. Of course, she might have done this intentionally. What do you think? On the back of the painting there's a small sketch of the house. Maybe she didn't like that drawing so she decided to have another try on the other side.

★ WHY IS THE PAINTING IMPORTANT IN THIS AREA?

There isn't a lot belonging to Mary Augusta in the Point Ellice collection because she died so young. This piece tells us a little about a young girl, whose story might be forgotten if not for the painting. Looking at this painting, we can imagine what her life was like and what made her happy.

CONNECTIONS

People have expressed themselves through art since the beginning of history. The oldest cave paintings are in the Magura Cave in northwest Bulgaria and were made between 10,000 and 8,000 years ago. Bat guano – that's a fancy name for bat poop – was used as paint. There are over 700 paintings in the cave. These can be divided into four categories: **geometric**, animals, symbols and anthropomorphic – this is what we call giving human qualities to nonhumans. A lot of cartoons do this. The paintings show shapes like zigzags and chessboard patterns, in addition to scenes from religious **rites**, fertility dances and hunting ceremonies, plants, animals and the stars, as well as **deities**.

JUST THE FACTS

BLUE AND WHITE CHAMBER POT

WHAT IS IT? A chamber pot was used at night because there were very few indoor toilets.

WHAT DOES IT LOOK LIKE? This white **porcelain** chamber pot looks like a giant's teacup, with a rounded bowl and handle. It's decorated with a molded turquoise ribbon around the rim. The bottom is stamped with a Chinese character. The year is shown with a *K*. This means it was made in 1883. This is quite different from the modern toilets we use today.

WHERE DOES IT COME FROM? The original owners of the house probably purchased the chamber pot. Peter and Caroline O'Reilly probably bought it while on a trip to England. The museum bought it as part of a collection from their grandson, John.

WHO USED IT? Every member of the O'Reilly household would have kept a chamber pot under their bed at night in case they had to use the toilet. Imagine keeping your toilet under your bed.

WOULD YOU BELIEVE?

Until the Victorian era, there were no public toilets for women. Before that time, women were afraid to go far from home in case they needed the bathroom. Some might have chosen not to eat or drink if they were out in public. Sometimes, if they couldn't hold it, they would pee in the gutter using their long skirts for privacy.

Tell Me More

The chamber pot is part of a set kept in Kathleen O'Reilly's room. Sets like hers often featured a wash basin, a water jug, a slop bucket, a soap dish, a sponge bowl and a toothbrush holder. These items helped people stay clean. The O'Reillys did have a tub, but to fill it up would take a long time, so they bathed less frequently than we do today. In between baths they cleaned themselves with a cloth and a wash basin. Afterwards the dirty water was taken away in the slop bucket and emptied into the soak pit, an underground structure made to absorb unwanted water. The chamber pot would be emptied in the morning into the outhouse or cesspool by the household help.

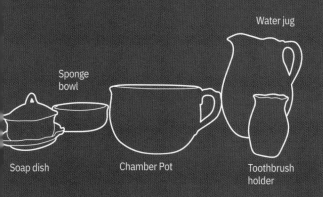

Water jug

Sponge bowl

Soap dish

Chamber Pot

Toothbrush holder

My Turn

Take a moment to think about the things you use every day that weren't around when your great-great-grandparents were kids.

CONNECTIONS

The ancient Romans were known for their modern public bathrooms. These were for men only and built using long benches with holes cut into them. By AD 315, the city of Rome had a whopping 144 public toilets. Romans weren't shy about using the bathroom with friends either. It was considered usual. There were no stalls. They might even sit and chat while doing their business. When they were finished, instead of reaching for the toilet paper, they reached for a stick with a sponge at the end of it that was then rinsed in water. Sometimes these sponges were kept in a mixture of vinegar and salt water. We may not have the same hygiene practices nowadays, but archeologists have found graffiti in these ancient bathrooms, proving some habits don't change!

WHY IS THE CHAMBER POT IMPORTANT IN THIS AREA?

There were no flushing toilets in 1867 when the O'Reillys moved into Point Ellice House. The first flush toilet in Victoria was said to have been in an Oak Bay residence on Simcoe Street, built in 1885.

WALKING TOUR
OF IMPORTANT VICTORIA MONUMENTS CONNECTED TO BLACK SETTLERS

Photo: Alwynne Ling

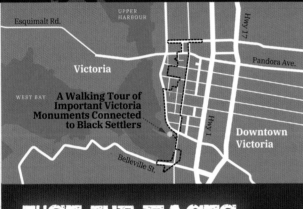

UPPER HARBOUR

Esquimalt Rd.

Victoria

Pandora Ave.

WEST BAY

A Walking Tour of Important Victoria Monuments Connected to Black Settlers

Hwy 17

Hwy 1

Downtown Victoria

Belleville St.

JUST THE FACTS

WHERE IS IT? Throughout the city of Victoria. For more information about Black settlers on Vancouver Island, visit **bcblackhistory.ca/learning-centre/places-of-interest-guide/.**

ARE PHOTOGRAPHS ALLOWED? Yes.

HOW DID IT START? This book is dedicated to giving everyone a chance to tell their unique story. During our research for this book, we learned about the BC Black History Awareness Society and its partnership with Digital Museums Canada. It wanted to make sure the stories of the Black settlers were not forgotten, so in the absence of a physical museum of Black history on Vancouver Island, it decided to draw attention to monuments associated with the settlers.

WHERE HAS IT LIVED?

The places mentioned in this section are the commemorative plaque in honour of the arrival of Black settlers at Victoria Harbour; the engraved bricks commemorating Victoria's settlers and pioneers at Bastion Square and 1000 to 1150 Government Street; the Mifflin Wistar Gibbs commemorative plaque in Irving Park in James Bay; Dandridge House located at 1243 Rudlin Street; and the Douglas Obelisk located in the gardens of BC's legislature.

WHERE DO THE ITEMS COME FROM?

These monuments are the work of people who wanted to keep history alive. They pay tribute to the contributions of Black settlers and remind us of the courage it takes to emigrate and leave a place one understands to travel to the unknown.

HOW HAS IT CHANGED?

Organizations like the BC Black History Awareness Society are working hard to make sure that Black history in BC is remembered. The society, which began in the early 1990s but was re-energized in the early 2000s, celebrates Black history in many ways, including recognizing the achievements of Black people through commemorative plaques.

HISTORIC DANDRIDGE HOUSE

The house is located at 1243 Rudlin Street, in Victoria, and belonged to John and Charlotte Dandridge. They came to Victoria as part of the 700 Black settlers invited by Governor James Douglas.

Dandridge House was built in 1861 on the northwest corner of Johnson and Vancouver streets. It was moved in 1897 to Rudlin Street. Imagine what a big job it would be if you decided to move your entire house.

The pretty, two-story homestead house looks like the perfect picture book house. It has three windows in the front and a large window downstairs. There's a covered veranda that John and Charlotte may have enjoyed sitting on.

Governor James Douglas is often referred to as the "Father of British Columbia." Before Douglas was the governor, he worked for the Hudson's Bay Company. In its records he's described as being Scotch West Indian. He was born in Demerara, British Guiana, which is now Guyana.

The settlers were determined to be part of their new community, and many became active in **colonial** and **municipal elections**. One member of the group, Mifflin Wistar Gibbs, was elected to the city council. Later he returned to the United States and became the first African American judge in the United States. He was also appointed United States consul to Madagascar.

It's not clear what John Dandridge did for a living. Some records say he was a waiter, others say he was a labourer.

The Black settlers Douglas invited arrived in Victoria just around the same time as the gold rush began in the Fraser River. Some decided to seek their fortune, but many remained in town, working as merchants, saloon keepers and barbers.

JUST THE FACTS

FORT VICTORIA BRICK PROJECT

WHAT IS IT? A memorial that celebrates Victoria's pioneers.

WHAT DOES IT LOOK LIKE? The project outlines the shape of Fort Victoria with a thousand coloured double bricks inscribed with the name of a pioneer.

WHERE DOES IT COME FROM? It was begun by the Greater Victoria Civic Archives Society.

WHO USED IT? Fort Victoria, originally known as Fort Camosun, was built for the Hudson's Bay Company in 1843. French Canadian employees of the company did the heavy work. The cedar logs used for the fort's **palisades** came from around Mount Douglas and were traded by the people of the Songhees Nation. It wasn't a fair trade though. Only one HBC blanket was provided for every 40 logs. The fort was created as a trade and **political** centre. It was also positioned well to show the Americans that the land was claimed.

Tell Me More

Included in this project are many Black pioneers. One of these people is Sylvia Estes Stark. She and her family arrived in Victoria around 1858–1859 with the other Black settlers invited by James Douglas. This amazing woman lived to be 105 years old. Sylvia was born into slavery in Missouri, the youngest of three children. Her mother worked for a baker called Charles Leopold and her father was a cowboy. He worked for a man called Thomas Estes. When she was about 10, Sylvia's father bought his family's freedom. He earned the money prospecting for gold. It cost $3,900. Back then, that was more than the average politician's allowance.

WOULD YOU BELIEVE?

In Missouri, when Sylvia Estes Stark was growing up, it was **illegal** *for Black children to learn to read and write. The penalties were steep – fines and time in jail for anyone caught teaching someone. Sylvia learned to read by listening as the children she looked after were taught.*

My Turn

Take a moment to think about what your life would be like if you weren't allowed to learn. Can you imagine not knowing how to read? What activities would you miss? What couldn't you do?

Nobel Peace Prize laureate, Malala Yousafzai grew up in Pakistan, a country where having a son is often considered more important than having a daughter. Malala's father didn't think that way. He was a teacher and a believer in education. He encouraged her to learn. She loved going to school. When she was 11 years old, an **extremist** group called the **Taliban** took over the town. They banned lots of different things like music and TV. Its leader commanded all education for females to stop.

In an interview with a famous TV presenter, Malala spoke up, saying girls had the right to learn. The Taliban didn't like this, so it had her shot. Luckily for Malala, she was well known, so she got the very best of care and survived. Today she's an Oxford University graduate. She runs an international charity dedicated to making sure all girls have the chance to an education.

WHY IS THE BRICK PROJECT IMPORTANT IN THIS AREA?

The bricks serve to remind us of all the different people who came to settle here. People from all sorts of circumstances and places throughout the world. By remembering them, we strengthen our community. We learn about local characters that we might not learn about at school. The bricks remind us that these people once walked the same streets, and, like us, had worries, friends and things they enjoyed.

JUST THE FACTS

WHAT IS IT? Brick No. 2232 is dedicated to the Black settlers Charles and Nancy Alexander who answered Sir James Douglas's call for colonists.

WHAT DOES IT LOOK LIKE? The brick is pink and engraved with the couple's names. It's located at 1120 Government Street.

WHERE DOES IT COME FROM? The Greater Victoria Civic Archives Society came up with this idea to commemorate the city's settlers.

WHO USED IT? In 1858, when Charles and Nancy Alexander arrived in Victoria with their two children, it was still a city of tents. Here their first home was a tent where the Hudson's Bay Company would one day stand.
    Both Charles and Nancy were born **Free Black** in St. Louis, Missouri. Charles worked as a prospector, farmer and carpenter. When their second child tragically died, they decided to move to California and work the goldfields.

Tell Me More

Returning from the goldfields to Victoria, Charles soon became recognized for his considerable skill as a carpenter. He is known for working on the first school in South Saanich, an area just outside Victoria, and the first Shady Creek Church at East Saanich Road and the Patricia Bay Highway. He was also a gifted speaker and often worked as a **lay preacher**.

Nancy was also an active member of the church and a member of the Lakehill Women's Institute, which held classes on health, cooking, weaving and hat making. The couple had 12 children, as well as a farm. In 1992 it was discovered the couple had 400 **descendants**.

CHARLES AND NANCY ALEXANDER, BRICK NO. 2232

WOULD YOU BELIEVE?

Charles and Nancy's great-grandson, James Douglas "Doug" Hudlin, was famous for his love of baseball. He was a well-known Victoria umpire for 40 years and was the first non-American to be invited to umpire the Little League World Series. Many other honours followed through the years, including induction into the Canadian Baseball Hall of Fame in 2017. In addition to this, he was the founding director of the BC Black History Awareness Society.

One of the couple's descendants, Kevin Alexander, is known as the "Gretzky of the Lacrosse Floor," and is famous for being one of the game's big goal scorers. For most of his career in the Western Lacrosse Association, he played with the Victoria Shamrocks. In 1991 he was **inducted** into the Canadian Lacrosse Hall of Fame.

My Turn

Listen to a direct descendant of Charles and Nancy talk about their legacy at Digital Museums Canada's Community Stories, "BC's Black Pioneers: Their Industry and Character Influenced the Vision of Canada," courtesy the BC Black History Awareness Society (https://www.communitystories.ca/v2/bc-black-pioneers_les-pionniers-noirs-de-la-cb/).

★ WHY IS BRICK NO. 2232 IMPORTANT IN THIS AREA?

The Alexanders were a big part of the creation of Victoria and its surrounding areas. They helped shape the construction, **commerce**, **culture** and religious life of the **region**. Their children, grandchildren, great-grandchildren and great-great-grandchildren have also had huge roles. They are a major part of the region's history.

City of Victoria Archives

JUST THE FACTS

WHAT IS IT? A plaque in Victoria's Inner Harbour honouring the arrival, in 1858, of the first group of Black settlers to the colony of Vancouver Island. It was erected by the Council of the City of Victoria. It's the second bronze plaque in a series of 71 paying tribute to major historic events that took place there.

WHAT DOES IT LOOK LIKE? A greenish-blue plaque with raised letters attached to the wall facing the harbour.

WHERE DOES IT COME FROM? The Council of the City of Victoria put it up on August 18, 1978.

WHO USED IT? In 1858 Governor James Douglas gave Jeremiah Nagle, captain of the British ship *The Commodore*, an important task. He sent him to San Francisco to invite members of the Black community to move to Victoria. Many of them were eager to flee the injustices they faced in their daily lives in California.

Sir James Douglas (1803–1877), Governor of British Columbia

PLAQUE 02 BLACK MIGRATION

IN COMMEMORATION OF THE ARRIVAL
IN 1858 OF THE FIRST GROUP O
BLACK SETTLERS TO THE COLONY O
VANCOUVER'S ISLAND.

THIS PLAQUE IS ERECTED BY THE COUNCIL O
THE CITY OF VICTORIA.

Tell Me More

The potential settlers met with Nagle at the First African Methodist Episcop Zion Church and he told them of the governor's offer. Immediately it was decided they'd send a group with Nagle and check out the offer. The group returned with g news: land was cheap, and they'd enjoy political and **economic** freedom.

Soon the Black settlers were on their way. They were the first group of non-British settlers to move to the colony. It was a good fit since they spoke English and knew what to expect of the society. They did all different kinds of work. Some of the settlers moved to areas like Salt Spring Island and farmed. Others preferred to pa the Fraser River for gold.

WOULD YOU BELIEVE?

Sadly, the Black settlers still faced racism from their new neighbours. In some churches they were forced to sit separately. Frequently, theatres refused them entry, or only allowed them seating in some areas. At saloons they were often overcharged or refused service. They were even forbidden from joining the volunteer fire department.

My Turn

Imagine you had to leave your home and move to another country. What would you miss the most, the place or the people? When you think of *home*, what is the first thing that springs to mind? A smell? A certain food? A parent's smile?

A Vietnam War–era draft card.
Source: Wikipedia, en:User:Lycurgus

CONNECTIONS

In the 1960s and 1970s, another group of Americans came to Canada: the Vietnam War draft dodgers. They were young men, usually well educated. They believed serving in the military should be a choice. They didn't think they should have to serve in a war all the way over in Vietnam that they didn't agree with or support. Many of them thought the war in Vietnam was none of their government's business. Some of them were pacifists. Pacifists are people who feel there is not a time when fighting is right. They came to Canada instead of going to war or being punished for refusing. Some Canadians helped the new arrivals. The United Church of Canada donated money to Toronto groups helping the draft dodgers. After the American government granted **amnesty** to the draft dodgers in 1977, many of them stayed in Canada. These men made important contributions in all parts of our society.

⭐ WHY IS THE PLAQUE IMPORTANT IN THIS AREA?

When people visit this part of the harbour and see the plaque, it teaches them about an important part of the city's history. It also reminds them that British Columbia is a province made up of lots of different experiences and voices. This is what makes it such a special place.

JUST THE FACTS

WHAT IS IT? A plaque dedicated to the Black settler Mifflin Wistar Gibbs, located in Irving Park in the James Bay area of Victoria.

WHAT DOES IT LOOK LIKE? A purple-red plaque, with raised gold letters, decorated with the emblem of Canada attached to a large piece of stone. The writing is in both English and French.

WHERE DOES IT COME FROM? It was **commissioned** by the Historic Sites and Monuments Board of Canada.

WHO USED IT? Dr. Verna Gibbs, Mifflin's great-great-grandniece, unveiled this plaque on May 4, 2019, with Mayor Lisa Helps in a ceremony held at Irving Park. Dr. Verna Gibbs travelled all the way from San Francisco for the tribute. The area was chosen for the plaque because James Bay was Mifflin's neighbourhood. He had a huge influence on his community, acting as their councillor for three years.

MIFFLIN WISTAR GIBBS COMMEMORATIVE PLAQUE

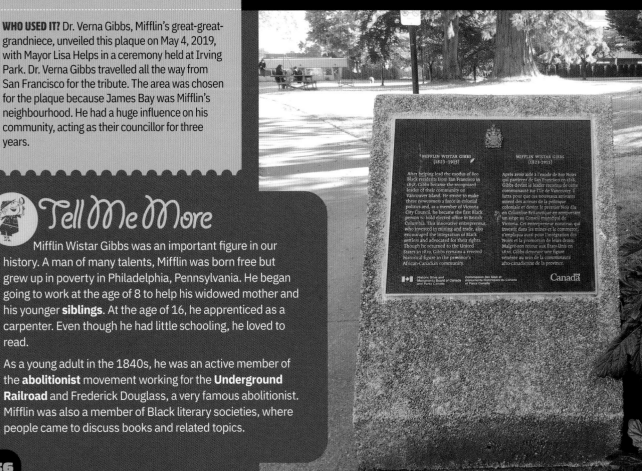

Tell Me More

Mifflin Wistar Gibbs was an important figure in our history. A man of many talents, Mifflin was born free but grew up in poverty in Philadelphia, Pennsylvania. He began going to work at the age of 8 to help his widowed mother and his younger **siblings**. At the age of 16, he apprenticed as a carpenter. Even though he had little schooling, he loved to read.

As a young adult in the 1840s, he was an active member of the **abolitionist** movement working for the **Underground Railroad** and Frederick Douglass, a very famous abolitionist. Mifflin was also a member of Black literary societies, where people came to discuss books and related topics.

My Turn

Think about how we group people. For example: "That kid sings in the choir; the kid over there is good at sports; those kids all speak a second language." What are your groups? What do people get wrong about these groups? What do people suppose about you because you like a certain thing? What's wrong with this kind of thinking?

CONNECTIONS

On June 10, 1957, Douglas Jung became the first elected Chinese Canadian Member of Parliament. This was a huge accomplishment considering that when he was born in 1924 Chinese Canadians didn't have any status.

Douglas grew up in a country where Chinese Canadians had to carry identity cards and weren't allowed to practise law or medicine, and couldn't live in certain neighbourhoods.

In 1939, during the Second World War, Douglas enlisted in the army. He thought this might trigger the government to change. He didn't get an assignment for a long time. The government didn't want to be forced into allowing Chinese Canadians equality. In 1944 Douglas and a group of other Chinese Canadians became part of Force 136, a branch of the British Special Operations Executive. The idea was to send them to Southeast Asia where they'd work against the Japanese.

After the war, Chinese Canadians were finally given the right to vote. Douglas went to university and became a lawyer. Four years later, he became a Member of Parliament.

WHY IS THE PLAQUE IMPORTANT IN THIS AREA?

Mifflin played an important role in the creation of Victoria and the province of BC. He is a much-admired historical figure in Canadian history. Over his lifetime, he was a community leader who led 600–800 Black settlers from California to British Columbia, the publisher of the *Alta California*, the only Afro-American newspaper, and the first Black person elected to public office in British Columbia in 1866. In 2016 the City of Victoria

marked his importance by declaring November 19 Mifflin Wistar Gibbs Day. Fittingly, given Mifflin's passion for reading, a meeting room in the James Bay Library Branch was named the Mifflin Wistar Gibbs Study Room.

Gibbs in 1902
Source: Wikipedia, Charles Milton Bell – C.M. Bell Studio Collection (Library of Congress)

JUST THE FACTS

THE DOUGLAS OBELISK

WHAT IS IT? A marble obelisk. It's like a statue but it doesn't have a sculpture of a person, animal or thing. Marble is a very special stone that costs a lot of money. An obelisk is a pillar that ends with a point. This one stands on the lawn of the British Columbia Parliament Buildings in Victoria.

WHAT DOES IT LOOK LIKE? It's eight metres tall. That's about the height of four men stacked on top of each other.

WHERE DOES IT COME FROM? It was made to honour Sir James Douglas, the governor and commander-in-chief of the colonies of Vancouver Island and British Columbia from 1851 to 1864.

WHO USED IT? Sir James Douglas played a huge part in making sure British Columbia was not annexed by the Americans after the Hudson's Bay Company left.

Tell Me More

The governor was born in British Guiana, now known as Guyana. His father, John Douglas, was a Scottish merchant who managed his family's plantation in Guyana. His mother, Martha Ann Ritchie, was born in Barbados a free woman of colour – a term used to describe a woman of African and European **heritage** who was not a slave.

Sir James had a brother, Alexander, and a sister, Cecilia. His parents never married. During this period in history, this was considered scandalous. When he was only 9 years old, his father took him to Scotland to be educated. Can you imagine travelling so far away from your home to go to school?

CONNECTIONS

In ancient Egypt, obelisks were called *tekhenu*, meaning to pierce. Maybe the Egyptians thought these gorgeous pieces would one day pierce the sky. The structures were known for their square base and narrow triangular pointed tops, similar in shape to a needle point.

The ancient Egyptians' first obelisks were not tall, only about three metres – that's about the size of two of the pop singer Ariana Grande put together. Eventually, this would change and some would be ten times as tall. One of the things that made these obelisks special is that they were made using a single piece of stone called monolith.

In Paris, at the Place de la Concorde, there's an ancient Egyptian obelisk that once stood during the time of Ramesses II as part of a pair outside the Luxor Temple. This is just one of the 28 remaining Egyptian obelisks still standing; of these only six of the remaining obelisks are in Egypt. The rest are around the world. Some, like the Parisian obelisks, were gifts from the Egyptian government, while others were stolen by invaders.

This is the Pylon of the Temple of Luxor in Egypt
Source: Wikipedia. Photo: Olaf Tausch

WHY IS THE DOUGLAS OBELISK IMPORTANT IN THIS AREA?

Sir James is often remembered as the "Father of British Columbia." It was because of his efforts that British Columbia became the sixth province of Canada. Sir James sent the invitation to San Francisco inviting the Black settlers to British Columbia. He wasn't a perfect leader though. He was known for being bad tempered and favouring his family and friends with jobs. Can a person be good and bad at the same time? What do you think?

5 THE MARITIME MUSEUM OF BRITISH COLUMBIA

Esquimalt Rd.
WEST BAY
Wharf St.
Hwy 1
Hwy 17
Pandora Ave.
Fairfield Rd.
Maritime Museum of British Columbia
Victoria

JUST THE FACTS

WHERE IS IT? 634 Humboldt Street, Victoria, BC, V8W 1A4; (250) 385-4222
mmbc.bc.ca

ARE PHOTOGRAPHS ALLOWED? Yes, but no flash, please!

HOW DID IT START? The idea for a museum began with local naval officers who wanted to preserve the navy history of the west coast of Canada. After many years of hard work, this group got support from Prince Philip, Duke of Edinburgh, which helped with the final push of **establishing** a museum here. While on a trip with then Princess Elizabeth to the naval base in Esquimalt, Prince Philip asked about a naval museum. Since there was none at the time, the prince worked to help start one. When he returned to England, he wrote to the National Maritime Museum in Greenwich, England, asking it to donate some of its items to help start the museum on this coast. These early donations are still in the collection today.

WHERE HAS IT LIVED?

In 1965 the museum moved to the home of the former Supreme Court in Bastion Square, the oldest surviving courthouse in British Columbia. In ten short years, the museum had outgrown its first home. By 2014 the old courthouse needed a great deal of work, so the museum was forced to find a new home. It settled on its current site. It's here that the museum has exhibitions and a research space. It keeps a large part of its collection off-site. These items are still available to the public through its research request program.

The museum hosts talks and craft workshops for the public, as well as a range of educational programs on topics like pirates and privateers, women at sea and the fur trade – just imagine what you could learn!

WHERE DO THE ITEMS COME FROM?

They were all donated.

HOW HAS IT CHANGED?

Although the museum originally just collected and **stewarded** naval materials, it has expanded its collecting practices to all things BC maritime—related, including natural history specimens, ocean plastics and shipbuilding, among others. The Maritime Museum of British Columbia also runs a variety of programs and continues to evolve to fit the changing needs of its **diverse** communities.

imagine adventures on the high seas

DOROTHY, THE OLDEST SAILING VESSEL IN THE PACIFIC NORTHWEST

Dorothy was built in 1897 by a talented shipbuilder called John J. Robinson in his James Bay boatyard, an area of Victoria, for around $1,800. William H. Langley, a well-known lawyer and member of the legislature, commissioned the boat.

Her most striking feature is her six-foot (1.8-metre) overhanging **fantail**. That's about 7.62 centimetres taller than the average Canadian man.

BC's Parliament Buildings and *Dorothy* are the same age.

She has beautifully kept logbooks. A ship's logbook tells the story of all the important events that took place on her. A logbook is like a person's diary, a record of the experiences that make up who one is, or in this case a record of this vessel's wild adventures. If we were to read about your life, what would we learn?

Linton Hope, a naval architect in England, designed *Dorothy*. Linton was an Olympian who won a gold medal for sailing in 1900 in Paris, France.

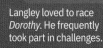

Langley loved to race *Dorothy*. He frequently took part in challenges.

Dorothy was built with all local wood. Both her **keel** and **framing** are made of oak. Her **hull** planks are made of western red cedar. *Dorothy* is famous for her beauty.

Today *Dorothy* is on Gabriola Island being restored by Tony Grove, who is a **shipwright**, a marine artist and a builder of fine furniture.

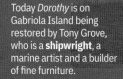

JUST THE FACTS

DOROTHY'S BELL

WHAT IS IT? *Dorothy*'s brass ship bell engraved with her name.

WHAT DOES IT LOOK LIKE? The bell looks like an upside-down bucket. Inside there's a clapper. When this is hit with a stick, the bell rings. Attached to the clapper is a piece of nautical ropework. The word "nautical" means things to do with sailors or navigating. Ropework refers to making and fixing ropes, as well as tying knots. It was common to decorate bells so they could be rung easily. Ropework was popular with sailors. They even decorated objects like telescopes. It was used as a way to judge and show off a sailor's skill.

WHERE DOES IT COME FROM? It was a working ship's bell until it was taken into the museum's care. It was donated to the museum in 1995.

WHO USED IT? The bell was used by *Dorothy*'s first owner, William H. Langley, and passed on with the vessel with each sale.

*Sailors have lots of superstitions. They believe it's bad luck to change a ship's name because when a ship is **christened** its name is put in the Ledger of the Deep. The deep is another name for the sea. This ledger belongs to the powerful Roman god of the sea, Neptune. Renaming a ship makes Neptune think he's being tricked, and that makes him mad.*

My Turn

In the past, sailors on long sea journeys survived on a rock-hard biscuit made from flour, water and salt called hardtack. It was so hard to chew it was nicknamed "the molar breakers," as well as "sea biscuit "and "ship's biscuit." Interested in learning how to make this survival food? Visit Herreshoff Marine Museum to learn how (https://herreshoff.org/2020/04/a-recipe-for-hardtack/).

Tell Me More

Ship's bells were used for telling time, as well as marking the hours of a sailor's watch schedule. This is a system that makes it possible for a ship to run all day and night and always have a sailor on duty, while at the same time allowing the other members of the crew to have a break. On a ship there are eight bells per shift. A bell rings every half-hour in a four-hour shift.

The job of keeping time was carried out by the boatswain (or bo's'n), who was also responsible for supervising the crew. On a smaller vessel like *Dorothy*, the bell also had other purposes, such as communicating with other ships during poor weather conditions. This was important, as radio communication was not very common when *Dorothy* was built in 1897.

Eight Bells (1887)
by Winslow Homer
Source: Wikipedia via Flickr

WHY IS THE BELL IMPORTANT IN THIS AREA?

A ship's bell is as unique as a person's fingerprint. Often it's the only way of identifying a ship after a shipwreck. After a ship was broken up or scrapped, the bell would be the only piece of the vessel that would be saved. As this bell is *Dorothy*'s bell, it's as if it's part of her body, and an important part of the area's history.

A long-time tradition of sailors and their families is the custom of **baptizing** the children of the ship's crew under, or in, the ship's bell – depending on the baby or the bell's size. Often the children's names and their baptismal dates were recorded on the bell. This was believed to be an honour, as a ship's bell was such a vital part of equipment.

JUST THE FACTS

WOODEN ROCKING CRADL RESEMBLING A SMALL BOAT

WHAT IS IT? A one-of-a-kind wooden cradle made to look like a small boat, commissioned by Captain Andrew Laing.

WHAT DOES IT LOOK LIKE? The cradle is made out of dark wood. The sleeping area, which is suspended between the two turned posts, looks just like a regular boat, except smaller. It's made to rock so the baby falls asleep. It might feel like falling asleep on a boat being rocked by the waves. At first glance, it might look like it would be uncomfortable, but it would have been lined with cushions and blankets.

WHERE DOES IT COME FROM? John J. Robinson built it in 1884. Robinson was the same man who built *Dorothy*, the oldest sailing vessel in the Pacific Northwest, our featured item.

WHO USED IT? It was used to cradle Captain Andrew Laing's four daughters. In 1961 his youngest daughter, Elizabeth, donated it to the museum.

? WOULD YOU BELIEVE?

This cradle was not an original idea. Back in his native England, Captain Andrew Laing had commissioned three similar cradles just like this for his older children. They weren't all the same, some had rockers installed on the underside of the hull. Others were built between posts like this one. Sadly, the others have not been preserved.

My Turn

Learn how to make your own boat. There's lots of instructional videos on YouTube. One of our favourites is "DIY Fantastic Floating Boat Created Using Recycled Material" (https://www.youtube.com/watch?v=UTFcjq8hw3c).

Tell Me More

This cradle is unusual because of the way the boards are fastened together. It's the same way that Vikings built their boats many years ago. The Vikings were famous shipbuilders who lived from the late eighth to the 11th century. The method is known as clinker built. *Clinker* is a Germanic word meaning fasten together. Today boatbuilders still use these ancient methods. In a place called Nydam, Denmark, archeologists found three ships built with this kind of construction. The largest ship is 23.5 metres long and 3.5 metres wide and dates to about AD 350. Imagine falling asleep in that!

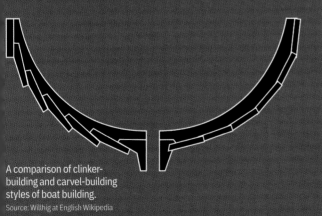

A comparison of clinker-building and carvel-building styles of boat building.
Source: Willhig at English Wikipedia

★ WHY IS THE CRADLE IMPORTANT IN THIS AREA?

It's a wonderful example of how the early families of the Pacific Northwest and the boatbuilding industry were connected and how boatbuilding was a way of life for these families. It also shows how many different skills are needed by boatbuilders. These skills can also be used to make other items, such as fine furniture and musical instruments.

CONNECTIONS

Viking children played with toy boats just like kids do today. The proof? In Orland, Norway, a wooden boat was discovered at an **Iron Age excavation site**. The boat is carved with a raised prow, and a hole in the middle for a mast. The boat would have been thought of as very cool. Back then it would be like having the newest and most expensive tablet or phone on the market.

6 BC FOREST DISCOVERY CENTRE

FOREST DISCOVERY CENTRE

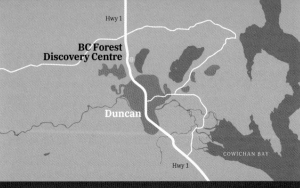

Hwy 1

BC Forest Discovery Centre

Duncan

COWICHAN BAY

Hwy 1

JUST THE FACTS

WHERE IS IT? 2892 Drinkwater Road, Duncan, BC, V9L 6C2; (250) 715-1113
bcforestdiscoverycentre.com

ARE PHOTOGRAPHS ALLOWED? Yes.

HOW DID IT START? This museum owes its existence to local businessman Gerry Wellburn. About 60 years ago, he decided to challenge people's notions about the lives of those working in the forest industry, as it bothered him that the community looked down on them. He did this by starting the Cowichan Valley Forest Museum, entertaining an impressive list of visitors, including Walt Disney.

WHERE HAS IT LIVED?

Gerry's museum was in his backyard at Deerholme, just outside of Duncan, BC. The museum attracted so many visitors that Gerry and his wife Ethel became overwhelmed, so Gerry began looking for a new home for it.

After discussions with local leaders, it was decided that the museum would stay in the Cowichan Valley, and the present site in Duncan was found. The location was perfect – close to the Island Highway and situated on beautiful Somenos Lake. As well, it's where the valley's first public building, a shared schoolhouse and chapel, once stood. In 1965 the museum opened, and visitors began riding the train around the museum's property.

WHERE DO THE ITEMS COME FROM?

The items come from Gerry's private collection. He was an incredible man with a gift for collecting. For years, long before the museum opened, he collected all sorts of items mostly from the forest industry, including steam "donkeys," locomotives, fire engines, bulldozers, logging trucks and even a post office. Today some of his items can be found in museums throughout British Columbia.

HOW HAS IT CHANGED?

Over the years there have been lots of changes. The museum's property has gotten bigger, the collection has grown and new exhibition areas have been created.

learn what it was like to work as a team

OLD FAITHFUL STEAM DONKEY

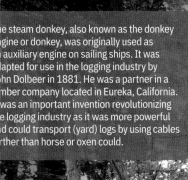

he steam donkey, also known as the donkey ngine or donkey, was originally used as n auxiliary engine on sailing ships. It was dapted for use in the logging industry by ohn Dolbeer in 1881. He was a partner in a mber company located in Eureka, California. was an important invention revolutionizing e logging industry as it was more powerful d could transport (yard) logs by using cables rther than horse or oxen could.

d Faithful was built by the ctoria Machinery Depot (VMD) in ctoria around 1914.

as Spratt, the owner of VMD, ed it at his estate in Deerholme, st south of Duncan, where the useum is located. During the rst World War, he built a sawmill ere.

the end of the war the sawmill as closed. Old Faithful was sold the Ferguson Bros., which erated it continuously for 40 ars at its logging operation.

The machine is important to the museum as very few steam donkeys have survived. Most were scrapped when more powerful steam and gas engines were introduced.

Old Faithful has a Boomerang Spark Arrester, located on its smokestack, which helps prevent forest fires, as required by the BC Forest Service.

This machine is a 25-horsepower unit. The term "horsepower" was invented by James Watt, a Scottish engineer. He lived in the 18th century and was famous for his work with steam engines. It's said the term "horsepower" was inspired by the ponies that worked in the mines. James wanted a way to describe how much work one of these ponies could complete in a minute.

Old Faithful weighs around 4500 kilograms, the average weight of an Asian elephant. This is also about the weight of a large male elephant seal.

JUST THE FACTS

WHAT IS IT? This building was part of the Model School complex from Vancouver, BC.

WHAT DOES IT LOOK LIKE? It looks like an old wooden house, which makes sense as it was built in 1905 by the BC Mills Timber & Trading Co. in Vancouver. The school is an early **prefabricated** or "ready-made" building that could be shipped to locations across western Canada for on-site assembly. Building plans for homes and city halls were also available. This school cost $550.00, and that included blackboards.

WHERE DOES IT COME FROM? The Model School's outbuildings were supposed to be demolished in 1985 by the Vancouver School Board, but luckily the Forest Discovery Centre managed to purchase the building for $1.00.

WHO USED IT? It was an elementary school that was used for student teachers to practise in while attending teacher training.

SCHOOL HOUSE

My Turn

If you were going to teach something, what would it be? Would you be able to be patient? How would you break it down? Do you think you'd be good at it? Teaching is very rewarding, so why not give it a try. The challenge: teach a friend or a parent how to do something you're an expert at that they've never tried before.

Tell Me More

This building has some very unique features. The sectional wall panels were constructed with layers of thin wood veneer and building paper on both the interior and exterior surfaces. These layers sandwiched dead space to act as insulation. This is pretty smart as schools can be pretty noisy places. The panels used to construct the building are interlocked and can be easily taken apart and stacked flat and shipped by railcar, the standard transportation used at that time. Very similar to the way things arrive from IKEA now!

Building the Eiffel Tower one piece at a time
Source: Wikipedia

WHY IS THE SCHOOLHOUSE IMPORTANT IN THIS AREA?

The schoolhouse is one of the most popular and important exhibits at the museum. It's open every day that the museum is open. Kids like to visit, hang out at the tables and colour. The schoolhouse is particularly popular at Halloween and Christmas, when the museum staff has crafts available for everyone. The only heat is from the wood stove in the corner. It keeps everyone lovely and warm. It also helps visitors to get a sense of what it was like to go to school in the past.

CONNECTIONS

Did you know the Eiffel Tower was built in only 22 months, from 1887 to 1889? How did its creator, Gustave Eiffel, manage to get the 300-metre-tall tower built so quickly? Yes, it was preassembled. The building was made from puddle iron from Pompey forges in the east of France. Puddling iron is a process that creates almost pure iron. The plates and beams that were made through this process were then preassembled in the Eiffel factories using rivets. Upon completion, these pieces were taken to the tower's construction site.

JUST THE FACTS

LOGGING CAMP COOKHOUSE

WHAT IS IT? This was where the meals were prepared for the loggers, and where they ate breakfast and dinner. Lunch was eaten in the forest.

WHAT DOES IT LOOK LIKE? It's a small wooden house painted blue with white trim. A standard design used by many logging camps, it was built on **foundation skids** that could be moved by railcar.

WHERE DOES IT COME FROM? The Victoria Lumber & Manufacturing Co. (later MacMillan Bloedel) built it in 1935 for its Copper Canyon Camp at Chemainus.

WHO USED IT? The kitchen staff – if the cook was a good cook, he was called a "mulligan mixer." If he was a bad cook, he was called a "bean burner," or a "can-opener artist." He was helped by the bullcook (a jack of all trades), the kitchen mechanic (the dish washer) and the flunkies (the dining hall servers and general kitchen help).

Tell Me More

The dinner bell, or the "guthammer," was rung by the cook to call the loggers to breakfast and dinner. At meals, seating was based on seniority; the most important people got the best seats. Meals were silent. The loggers consumed about 9,000 calories per day – that's a lot. Think about this: an average, growing, 12-year-old kid needs about 2,625 calories a day. The loggers were eating about three and half times more. Food was so important that the camp serving the best meals got the best men. In fact, the quality of food served was more important than how much a camp paid.

"Dark dining" is the idea that the smells and the flavours of a meal are more intense if we can't see what we are eating. It's a big trend, but it's more than just a cool way to eat; it can also make people more empathetic – meaning more understanding – of other people's feelings. It's thought that after spending a couple of hours in the dark, sighted people might begin to feel a tiny portion of what visually impaired people experience every day. The idea began with Jorge Spielmann, a blind pastor from Zurich, Switzerland, who set up a restaurant in a church in 1999 with four blind friends. The restaurant is named Blind Cow (*Blindkuh*), after the Swiss version of blindman's bluff. Customers eat in the dark and are served by blind and visually impaired servers. Since its founding, a second restaurant has opened in Basel, Switzerland.

My Turn

It's time for you to create your own lingo. What will you use as your inspiration? A favourite movie, a video game, or a sport? Once you've figured out what you're using, try it out on some friends and see their reactions.

⭐ WHY IS THE COOKHOUSE IMPORTANT IN THIS AREA?

The way a community eats tells us a lot about the lives they lived. The cookhouse is a window into the world of the logging camp. We can learn a lot about their daily routine by what they ate and how they ate. The way people sat in the dining hall tells us how people were ranked in this community.

As with your family and friends, eating together provided an opportunity for the loggers to come together, strengthen ties and build better relationships.

Mess Hall at Logging Camp
Source: Wikipedia

LOGGING CAMP BUNKHOUSE

JUST THE FACTS

WHAT IS IT? This is where the loggers slept, relaxed and kept their belongings.

WHAT DOES IT LOOK LIKE? On the outside it's exactly like the other buildings. Inside the floor is heavily marked from the men wearing their caulk (pronounced "cork") boots. These were leather boots made with spikes for walking on logs and slippery surfaces in the forest. Bunkhouses were heated by a woodstove in the middle of the building.

WHERE DOES IT COME FROM? Like the other buildings, it was built in 1935 by the Victoria Lumber & Manufacturing Co. (later MacMillan Bloedel) for its Copper Canyon Camp at Chemainus. It has the same construction as the cookhouse.

WHO USED IT? Bunkhouses were often **segregated** by nationality. Loggers came from all over the world: Europe, China and India. In some bunkhouses the common language might have been Mandarin or Hindi rather than English.

Tell Me More

The men lived in very cramped quarters, often eight to a room about the size of a large bedroom. Basically, if you turned over in your bed to sleep on your side you were facing someone. There were two rooms in each bunkhouse, so this meant 16 men per building. Can you imagine all the snoring and coughing? Would you be able to sleep?

The bunkhouses could also get rather smelly at times, with the smell of wet woolen clothes being hung up to dry and the housing of sweaty workers living in close quarters. Laundry was hung up to dry after a wet working day, or on laundry day, which was Sunday.

WOULD YOU BELIEVE?

The loggers wore canvas pants called "tin pants" as their outer layer of clothing. Developed in the early 1900s, these heavy cotton pants were treated with a combination of oil and wax to waterproof them. They'd let **pitch***, oil and grease build up on them to make the pants stiff and waterproof. Shirts were boiled in linseed oil to make them water resistant.*

The term "bunkhouse men" was used to describe Canadian workers who travelled from one remote place to another for work in the early 20th century. Often they worked in all-male environments as unskilled labour in industries like construction, mining, harvesting and logging. The bunkhouse men were usually single and often from other countries. They worked hard for their earnings and were often treated unfairly. For this reason, many became involved in the creation of **labour reforms unions**.

⭐ WHY IS THE BUNKHOUSE IMPORTANT IN THIS AREA?

The bunkhouse shows how different life as a logger was in the early to mid-century compared to today. Today there are very few of these buildings in existence. These were purchased by Gerry Wellburn in 1954 and moved to the Cowichan Valley Forest Museum in 1964, just before the museum's official opening.

My Turn

Robert Swanson was known as the "Bard of the Woods," for his ballads about logging on the BC coast. His work was so popular that in the 1980s he travelled around with a troupe that read and sang about logging. If you were going to write about your life, what form would it take? Would it be a poem? A rap? Or a pop song? Think about it.

Robert Swanson (1905–1994). Not only a logger, he was also a qualified locomotive engineer. He is credited with the invention of the first 5- and 6-chime air horn used on locomotives, which is what the strange horns are in this picture.

Photo: Brian Kent, Railway Appliance Research Collection, Nanaimo District Museum. Courtesy DieselDuck.info

JUST THE FACTS

STEAM LOCOMOTIVI
SHAWNIGAN LAKE LUMBER CO. NO. 2

WHAT IS IT? The Shawnigan Lake Lumber Co. No. 2 is a steam locomotive that was built in 1910 by Climax Locomotive Works in Corry, Pennsylvania.

WHAT DOES IT LOOK LIKE? It's painted black with red trim, and it has a number two painted on it. There's a chimney that looks like an upside-down vase, a large headlamp and a bell.

WHERE DOES IT COME FROM? Restored by Granger Taylor, it was purchased by the Province of BC and placed on display at the BC Forest Discovery Centre in 1980.

WHO USED IT? The Shawnigan Lake Lumber Company purchased this locomotive in 1910. After that it belonged to Sahtlam Lumber and, later, to Channel Logging. In 1930 it was **abandoned**.

WOULD YOU BELIEVE?

After the locomotive, Granger restored an old bulldozer and a Second World War P-40 Kitty Hawk airplane. Along with fixing up heavy antique transport and construction machinery, Granger had a keen interest in spaceships and space travel. At his family farm, he built a spaceship out of two satellite dishes with his friend Robert. Sadly, in 1980, Granger disappeared under unusual circumstances. A CBC documentary called Spaceman was made about him.

My Turn

Learn how to make your own steam engine with one of the fabulous videos on YouTube. You'll find everything from building a steam engine from a lawn mower, to building one from a soda can.

WHY IS THE LOCOMOTIVE IMPORTANT IN THIS AREA?

These huge machines were a dynamic part of the Vancouver Island logging industry from the 1900s to the 1950s. It's important that the part they played be remembered. Very few people know how much of the interior of the island was covered in tracks. Trucks brought an end to the use of trains, as they could maneuver steep terrain more easily.

Tell Me More

The locomotive No. 2 was salvaged and restored by Granger Taylor in 1969. From an early age, he showed an **aptitude** for mechanics and by his late teens had gained a reputation for being able to fix nearly anything. He found this locomotive when he was in his 20s. It was abandoned a few kilometres from his parents' home on the far side of Somenos Lake. It was rotting and falling apart. With the help of some friends, and the use of a truck, Granger managed to pull the 25-ton locomotive out of the forest. Granger worked for two years to restore the locomotive to its former glory.

CONNECTIONS

The first Canadian locomotive, the Dorchester, travelled from La Prairie and Saint-Jean-sur-Richelieu, Quebec, on Canada's first public railway, the Champlain and Saint Lawrence. Robert Stephenson and Company of Newcastle upon Tyne, England, built the locomotive in 1835. Robert was the son of George Stephenson, the man called the "Father of Railways." It arrived in Canada by barge and was put together. The Dorchester was almost four metres in length and weighed 5,114.25 kilograms.

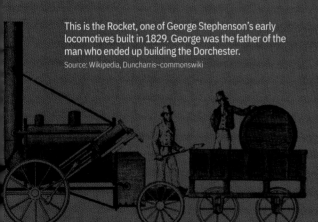

This is the Rocket, one of George Stephenson's early locomotives built in 1829. George was the father of the man who ended up building the Dorchester.

Source: Wikipedia, Duncharris~commonswiki

JUST THE FACTS

FILER'S SHOP (DENTIST'S SHOP)

WHAT IS IT? The (saw) filer's shack was a place where the **faller**'s saw was sharpened and repaired. Originally, filers would have worked on crosscut saws and then later chainsaws, which were introduced in 1936. Filers also sharpened other tools such as axes and knives.

WHAT DOES IT LOOK LIKE? On the outside, exactly like the other buildings. Inside there was a workshop where loggers could bring their saws to be sharpened. Back in the day, the air was probably quite dusty and smelled a bit like burned metal. There would be a workbench, a vice, a grindstone for axes and files of all sorts.

WHERE DOES IT COME FROM? The Victoria Lumber & Manufacturing Co. built it in 1935 for its Copper Canyon Camp at Chemainus. Later the forestry company MacMillan Bloedel owned it.

WHO USED IT? The filer aka "the dentist" worked here. He was called the dentist because the saws he repaired had teeth.

Tell Me More

The filer was highly skilled and well paid. The job was very busy. Crosscut saws were the most common saw used in the industry. There were two kinds of crosscut saws: two-person and one-person. It took a filer about half an hour to file a saw. They repaired about 20 a day. Some filers were very picky and wouldn't accept a saw that wasn't cleaned or still had **debris** on it. Filers sometimes gave loggers a hard time about not taking care of their saws.

CONNECTIONS

In the small towns of the Canadian west that followed the railway's route, the blacksmith, like the filer, was an important part of his community. His services were constantly in demand. If he wasn't shoeing horses, he was fixing farm machinery or a wagon wheel. In addition to this, he repaired tools used for fishing, forestry and transportation. In some communities the blacksmith also acted as the veterinarian and even as a doctor. In 19th- and 20th-century rural Quebec, there were even some blacksmiths who recommended medical treatments based on some superstitions, a little science and folklore.

Blacksmith's shop in Canada, late 19th Century
Wikimedia Commons

⭐ WHY IS THE FILER'S SHOP IMPORTANT IN THIS AREA?

The lumber industry was a key part of Canada's development as a country. The trade brought money, immigration and exploration, and it boosted the development of small towns. Learning about the roles people played in this industry is a central part of understanding who we are as a country.

Can you imagine what would happen if there were nobody to sharpen these huge saws? These are loggers in Oregon with a two-man crosscut saw.

Source: Wikipedia, Original Collection: Gerald W. Williams Collection, Item Number: WilliamsG:Ford 8

VANCOUVER ISLAND

Museum at Campbell River

Cumberland Museum and Archives

Qualicum Beach Museum

Alberni Valley Museum

Ucluelet Aquarium

THE MIDDLE

7 ALBERNI VALLEY MUSEUM

Photo courtesy of Alberni Valley Museum

JUST THE FACTS

WHERE IS IT? 4255 Wallace Street, Port Alberni, BC, V9Y 3Y6; (250) 720-2863
playinpa.ca/museum-2

ARE PHOTOGRAPHS ALLOWED? Photographs can be taken without flash.

HOW DID IT START? When the Alberni District Museum and Historical Society formed, it started collecting information and artifacts. Two years later, when Canada celebrated its **centennial**, Port Alberni also celebrated by building the Echo '67 Centre. It includes an aquatic centre, community centre, regional library and the museum and archives. The Alberni Valley Museum opened four years later in 1971. The museum is owned and operated by the city. There is also space for the historical society to maintain the archives.

WHERE HAS IT LIVED?

The museum has always lived in this building.

WHERE DO THE ITEMS COME FROM?

Most of the collection has been donated. People give their belongings to the museum so they are safe and can be taken care of, and so others can enjoy them and learn from them. When an item is donated, the museum asks for information about its history, who owned it and how it is connected to Port Alberni. Sometimes, but not very often, the museum purchases an artifact for the collection if it is important and buying it is the only way to save it and keep it in the community. The museum owns the majority of the collection. There are a few collections of archeological material that it holds **in trust** for the Nuu-chah-nulth First Nation.

HOW HAS IT CHANGED?

Like many others, the Alberni Valley Museum has temporary exhibits, which means there are always parts of the museum that are changing. Technology has also allowed a major change in the way people can visit the museum. You can now search the museum's photograph collection – over 22,000 photographs – online. You can also visit the galleries virtually.

Learn about a world-famous Canadian painter

EMILY CARR PAINTING OF SPROAT LAKE, BC

Photo courtesy of Alberni Valley Museum

Emily Carr is a famous Canadian artist and writer best known for her brightly coloured paintings of Indigenous totem poles, villages and west coast forests.

She painted Sproat Lake when she was visiting Klitsa Lodge in 1908. If you could sit in the front room of the lodge, this is what you'd see – the lake with Klitsa Mountain in the background.

It is painted in oil on a board about the size of a laptop. It's small because she had to carry all her materials with her.

In 1971 Canada Post reproduced one of Emily Carr's most famous paintings, *Big Raven*, on a six-cent stamp.

Because she was a woman, and her art was so original, she did not become well known until she was in her 50s.

Ralph Tieleman, an art collector who lived in Tofino, donated the painting to the museum in 2014.

Emily Carr loved animals. Wherever she lived, she always had animals with her – lots of dogs, cats, even a raccoon. But her most famous pet was Woo, her monkey.

Emily Carr was given the name Klee Wyck when she visited Ucluelet. In Nuu-chah-nulth the name means "Laughing One." Her first book, entitled *Klee Wyck*, won the Governor General's Award for nonfiction in 1941.

JUST THE FACTS

WHAT IS IT? This doll, handmade by John Halfyard, is a **fur trapper**.

WHAT DOES IT LOOK LIKE? The trapper wears a toque, scarf, fur mitts and boots, leather leggings, snowshoes and carries a backpack.

WHERE DOES IT COME FROM? Aileen Devereux first donated the doll to the Rollin Art Centre in Port Alberni. John lived with the Devereux family in the later part of his life. The Rollin Art Centre donated the doll to the museum. The centre worried it would not be able to look after it properly.

WHO USED IT? John created over 200 dolls in his lifetime. Many of them (including this one) stayed with him when they weren't being shown at other galleries or crafts festivals. Others he sold or gave away.

Tell Me More

John Halfyard had an unusual life. He was born on a small island off northern France, but when he was 7 years old, his parents abandoned him. He came to Canada as a young man and did many different jobs where he met interesting people, including circus performers and fur trappers. Because of a learning disability, he never learned to read, but he loved to tell stories – some of them true and some of them made up. He started making dolls when he was 84 and used fabrics left over from Mrs. Devereux's sewing and weaving projects. Many of the dolls – like the clowns and the trappers – were based on people he had met.

TRAPPER DOLL

Photo courtesy of Alberni Valley Museum

My Turn

If you were a reporter, what questions would you ask John Halfyard?

CONNECTIONS

When the famous French artist and sculptor Edgar Degas went blind, he still made doll-like wax figures of ballerinas. These little dancers were not found until after he died. They were made into bronze sculptures and are in galleries and museums around the world.

John Halfyard, with some of the many dolls he created.
Photo courtesy of Alberni Valley Museum

⭐ WHY ARE JOHN HALFYARD'S DOLLS IMPORTANT IN THIS AREA?

John's work teaches us many things. Even if you don't learn the same way as other people do, you can still explore the things you love. Age doesn't have to stop you from doing what you love. Finally, imagination and creativity can be part of everyone's life.

You can see John's creativity in this trapper doll. His hair and beard were made out of sheep's fleece. His mitts and boots were made from parts of a fur coat given to John by a local woman. For the snowshoes, he wrapped string over willow twigs. But to make them look real he dipped them in wax. If you could look inside the trapper's backpack, you would see a tiny metal frying pan and a blanket.

John's dolls can be found in many collections, including the Canadian Museum of History in Ottawa.

JUST THE FACTS

WHAT IS IT? *Piika-uu* means small useless or decorative basket.

WHAT DOES IT LOOK LIKE? It's a round, unfinished basket made of thin cedar bark strips covered with swamp grass. Some of the swamp grass is dyed different colours. The *basket* has many designs on it in black, red, green, orange and purple. The designs represent various fish, animals and birds important in our lives along the west coast of the island. You may recognize the eagle with a snake in its mouth.

WHERE DOES IT COME FROM? This basket came from Nuumaḳimyiis, a small First Nations village at the mouth of the Sarita River near Bamfield, where its last owner, Dora Frank, lived.

WHO USED IT? Dora Frank last owned this basket. She used to copy the designs on this old basket when she was weaving new baskets.

Tell Me More

Frank may not have made this basket. Most often pattern baskets were woven by older weavers and handed down to younger weavers when they first began making baskets. Weavers often set their pattern basket in front of them to see what colour of grass to use for each design and to see how many stitches there are in each row of the design. Then they choose that colour of grass and weave that number of stitches.

> ALBERNI VALLEY MUSEUM

PIIKA-UU (DECORATIVE BASKET)

BY HAA'YUUPS, HEAD OF THE HOUSE OF TAḲIISHTAḲAMLTHAT-ḥ, OF THE HUUPACH'ESAT-ḥ FIRST NATION

Photo courtesy of Alberni Valley Museum

WOULD YOU BELIEVE?

Some basket makers can weave an entire basket without looking at a pattern. They memorize the colour of grass and the number of stitches in every row of every design they use. Some women have woven baskets using strips of grass almost as fine as a human hair. Baskets which sold for 50 cents in 1920 are now worth thousands of dollars. Women used to weave baskets so tightly they could hold water. Baskets were sometimes filled with water and hot rocks and then cooked in.

My Turn

Study the designs on this basket for 90 seconds. Take note of the different animals, their positions and their colours. Now cover the photo and try to draw the designs on the basket as you remember them. Remove the cover. Compare your drawing. Study the photo again and, without looking at it, draw the designs again. How many times would it take for you to get the animals, the colours and the spacing just like they appear in the photo? Imagine how difficult it would be for a weaver to memorize all the colours and stitch counts!

Pattern baskets are like blueprints for boats. Shipwrights and carpenters follow blueprints when cutting wood or metal when building a boat. Pattern baskets are like recipes too. A baker follows a recipe, and if he copies it correctly, he makes good bread. Pattern baskets are most like knitting patterns because of the counting of stitches in a row. I have seen women copy knitting patterns onto baskets.

⭐ WHY IS THE PIIKA-UU IMPORTANT IN THIS AREA?

Pattern baskets are important as tools for use by weavers. Even the best weavers follow designs on their pattern baskets. Most of the weavers I grew up with said their pattern baskets were precious to them because they received them from their mothers, their aunts or their grandmothers. One old woman I talked to said she thought her pattern basket was priceless because, when she was just a little girl, an old woman with no children of her own wove it and gave it to her, asking her to remember her whenever she used the pattern basket. Pattern baskets are also important because they show the designs used by different tribes. Each tribe on the west coast has its own designs. Some designs show important events in the tribe's history.

Decorative baskets are produced all over the world. These are woven palm-frond and rush baskets, made in Yemen.
Photo: Davidbena, Wikipedia

SILVER TEA SET

JUST THE FACTS

WHAT IS IT? This tea set includes a teapot, a creamer, a sugar bowl and a tea waste (a place to put your used tea leaves).

WHAT DOES IT LOOK LIKE? The set is silver, and all the pieces have four little feet and a very fancy edge on the handles.

WHERE DOES IT COME FROM? A member of Minnie Paterson's family donated the set in 2010. They wanted to make sure Minnie's exciting story continued to be told.

WHO USED IT? What makes this ordinary object extraordinary is that, in 1907, the Seattle Maritime Union gave the set to Minnie Paterson for heroism. She helped save the crew of the ship *Coloma* when they almost lost their lives in a raging storm near Bamfield, BC.

Photos courtesy of Alberni Valley Museum

Tell Me More

Minnie Paterson lived in the Cape Beale lighthouse with her husband, Tomas the lighthouse keeper, and their children. The winds off Cape Beale on December 6, 1906, were almost 150 kilometres per hour. The lumber the *Coloma* carried on her deck broke free in the rough seas, smashing the **gunwhales** of the ship. Her sails ripped, and the main **mast** snapped off. The crew was helpless. Tom saw the ship from the lighthouse, but the telegraph line to Bamford – the closest town where he could get help – was down. He couldn't leave the lighthouse, so Minnie went instead.

My Turn

Now that you have read about Minnie Paterson and Viola Desmond, how has your thinking about heroism changed?

WOULD YOU BELIEVE?

Minnie made this whole journey in her husband's slippers. She thought they would be more flexible than boots. It took a few days before the telegraph lines were repaired. Only then did Minnie and Tomas discover that the rescue had been successful.

CONNECTIONS

Heroism doesn't necessarily mean saving lives. Some heroes are quiet. Viola Desmond, a Black woman born in Nova Scotia in 1914, was a successful businesswoman. One evening she went to a movie, choosing a seat on the main floor of the theatre. Unlike in the United States, Canada didn't have official **segregation** laws. But many businesses did. Viola was asked to move to the balcony where Black people were supposed to sit. She refused. The police charged Viola because the seats on the floor cost an extra cent and she had not paid the extra. She fought the charges all the way to the Supreme Court. While she lost the battle in court, her fight called attention to the unfair treatment of Blacks in Canada. You can see Viola Desmond's picture on the $10 bill. She is the first Black Canadian woman to be on our **currency**.

Viola Desmond, Halifax, Nova Scotia. circa 1940.
Source: Winnipeg Free press, authour unknown

⭐ WHY IS THE TEA SET IMPORTANT IN THIS AREA?

Minnie left the lighthouse with her dog, waded through waist-deep water and started toward Bamfield, eight kilometers away. She hoped to find a rowboat at Bamfield Creek, but it was gone. She ran as fast as she could through the bush, through mud and over slippery rocks to the home of James McKay. He wasn't there, but his wife, Annie, helped Minnie row a small boat through the crashing waves down the Bamfield inlet to get help from the *Quadra*, a boat that could rescue the *Coloma*. Minnie didn't rest. She rowed to the **cable station** in Bamfield to report the disaster. Then she walked back to the lighthouse to be with her infant son. Today Minnie's heroism would be all over the internet and journalists would be competing to interview her. But in those days this tea set would have been a cherished item to be proudly displayed in Minnie's home.

8 UCLUELET AQUARIUM

All photos courtesy of Ucluelet Aquarium

Ucluelet
Aquarium

Ucluelet

North Pacific Ocean

JUST THE FACTS

WHERE IS IT? 180 Main Street, Ucluelet, BC, V0R 3A0; (250) 726-2782
ucllueletaquarium.org

ARE PHOTOGRAPHS ALLOWED? Yes, but no flash please. The animals are sensitive to light.

HOW DID IT START? In 2004 Philip Bruecker decided to create a mini-aquarium in which each **species** collected would be let go when the aquarium closed in the fall. This idea was unique in Canada. All the species were collected locally and kept in tanks pumped through with sea water from the ocean just outside. When the aquarium closed for the season, the staff and members of the community returned the species to the sea.

WHERE HAS IT LIVED?

When the mini-aquarium opened in 2004, it was in a trailer at the end of the dock above the beach in Ucluelet. It became so popular that the original building became too small. In 2012 a new aquarium opened very close to the original site.

WHERE DO THE ITEMS COME FROM?

All the species are local. Some are hand-gathered by aquarium staff from beaches at low tide. Others are collected in shallow water by **snorkellers**. Fish or **invertebrates** that live in deep water are collected by expert divers who have a special licence. The main collection period is at the beginning of the year before the aquarium opens in March.

HOW HAS IT CHANGED?

The building where the aquarium now lives is the biggest change. But what's inside the aquarium also changes. What you see in the tanks one year might be different from the year before or the year after. If the collectors can't find a species, it won't be in the aquarium. Every year the number of specimens that leave the aquarium is greater than the number that came in. That's because fish **spawn** and have babies.

Other changes include the projects the aquarium is involved with. The staff works with universities and research societies to help study things like the amount of radiation in the ocean, and how diseases like sea star wasting syndrome are affecting different species. With help from "citizen scientists" (volunteers who work alongside scientists), the aquarium is tracking microplastics and marine debris on local beaches.

Meet an octopus with 9 brains!

GIANT PACIFIC OCTOPUS

Giant Pacific octopuses are the largest of all species of octopus. They can grow up to ten metres in three to five years. They are released from the aquarium after two or three months, before they can outgrow their tank.

Pacific octopuses are masters of disguise. Not only can they change the colour of their skin, they can change the **texture** from smooth to bumpy.

Because they have no skeletons, octopuses can fit into tiny places. Only their beaks – which look a little like a parrot's beak and are used to break the shells of crabs and clams – are hard. If their beaks can fit through a hole, so can their whole body!

hey have personalities. One year, hen an octopus was released om the aquarium, instead of wimming away, it crawled along e shallows with its **mantle** out of e water as if to say goodbye.

Not only do these **cephalopods** have a central brain that controls the **nervous system**, they have a brain in each arm that allows them to move their arms independently or together. That's nine brains in total!

They have a lifespan of three to five years. They weigh an average of 60 kilograms. Compare that to your weight.

Giant Pacific octopuses have three hearts and blue blood caused by a copper-rich **protein** called hemocyanin. This protein helps the blood carry oxygen at low water temperatures.

JUST THE FACTS

SEA STAR

WHAT IS IT? A sea star is a star-shaped invertebrate that lives in the ocean.

WHAT DOES IT LOOK LIKE? Most species have five arms. They have a central disk with overlapping plates that protect them. Many are brightly coloured.

WHERE DOES IT COME FROM? There are about 43 species in the waters surrounding Ucluelet. The most common ones include the ochre stars, leather stars, blood stars, mottled stars and bat stars. They live between the intertidal zone of the ocean, which is covered with water when the tide is high and uncovered at low tide, and depths of up to 6000 metres.

WHO USED IT? With sea stars, it's more of a "what" than "who." Sea stars are **keystone predators**. They play a big part in keeping the lower intertidal **ecosystem** balanced.

Tell Me More

There are about 2,000 species of sea stars in Earth's oceans. While many have five arms, some have many more. The sunflower star can have 15–24 arms, more than any other sea star. Imagine what you could do with that many arms. On their underside, sea stars have hundreds of tube feet that fill with water and help them move along the bottom of the ocean. The tough covering on their topside has spines that protect them from their enemies. They love to eat mussels, clams, small fish, snails and **barnacles**.

WOULD YOU BELIEVE?

When sea stars eat mussels, they use their tube feet to find an opening into the mussel's shell. Once they've found the opening, the sea star pushes its stomach through its mouth and into the shell. Digestive juices from the stomach dissolve the mussel's flesh.

CONNECTIONS

Climate change is connected to sea star wasting disease. The warming of our oceans has had an **impact** on these invertebrates. Scientists think that, with warmer water, there is more **organic material** like algae, which causes more bacteria. These bacteria consume oxygen around the sea stars, causing them breathing difficulties. Sea stars can't go to the doctor or pharmacy and get a shot or take a pill to prevent getting sick like we can. So as the ocean warms up, sea stars are more likely to struggle.

⭐ WHY IS THE SEA STAR IMPORTANT IN THIS AREA?

Sadly for local sea stars, a **virus** called sea star wasting syndrome was discovered in 2013. In 2015 the virus killed an estimated 96 per cent of sunflower sea stars off the central coast of British Columbia. The death of the sea stars has affected the balance in the ocean's ecosystem. Sunflower sea stars eat sea urchins, which is a good thing because sea urchins eat **kelp**. Because kelp forests are home to many fish, invertebrates and marine mammals, when kelp disappears, the **habitat** for these species is lost. Even humans use kelp. Many toothpastes, cosmetics, food and medicines contain kelp.

The Ucluelet Aquarium staff can't cure the virus, but they are doing monthly sea star surveys to keep track of the disease. Because the local sea star species live along the Pacific coast from northern California to southern Alaska, the aquarium staff work on this project with the Strawberry Isle Marine Research Society in Tofino, BC, and the University of California in Santa Cruz.

Sea Star eating a mussel
Wikimedia Commons: photo by Brocken Inaglory

› UCLUELET AQUARIUM

CHINOOK SALMON

JUST THE FACTS

WHAT IS IT? Chinook are the largest of the Pacific salmon. But the salmon you see in the aquarium will look very little. They are still young, only about 1 year old.

WHAT DOES IT LOOK LIKE? Adult chinook have blue-green heads and backs and silver sides. They grow to about 0.9 metres long and weigh around 13 kilograms. But before they become adults, these fish go through four stages: egg, **alevin**, **fry** and **smolt**.

WHERE DOES IT COME FROM? The salmon you see in the aquarium come from the Thornton Creek hatchery. The goal of the hatchery is to increase the **salmon runs** in the Barkley and Clayoquot sounds.

WHO USED IT? The aquarium uses these young salmon to teach visitors about the fish's life cycle and their importance to humans and to the environment.

WOULD YOU BELIEVE?

*Trees depend on salmon. When bears eat salmon, they drag them onto the shore. What they don't eat eventually becomes fertilizer, which feeds the plants and trees beside the river. These **marine nutrients** are what allow us to have such beautiful old-growth trees here in British Columbia.*

My Turn

As well as fish hatcheries, what things can you, your friends and your family do (or not do) to make sure we will still have lots of chinook salmon in the future?

Tell Me More

Chinook salmon are anadromous. That means they are born in freshwater rivers, spend their adult lives in saltwater oceans and then return to the river where they were born to lay their eggs. Most fish born in fresh water can't survive in salt water. The young chinook salmon don't swim immediately from fresh to salt water. They spend time in **estuaries** where the water is a mix of fresh and salt. This gives their bodies time to adapt to their new environment.

CONNECTIONS

As mentioned above, anadromous fish are born in fresh water and spend their adult lives in salt water. Some fish do the exact opposite. They are born in salt water, live their adult lives in fresh water and return to the sea to spawn and lay their eggs. These types of fish are called catadromous. The European eel is one example of this type of fish.

⭐ WHY IS THE CHINOOK SALMON IMPORTANT IN THIS AREA?

Chinook salmon play an important role in our ecosystem. They are a food source not just for humans but also for seals, killer whales and big birds of prey. Every April through October, adult chinook return to the rivers where they were born, and bears are ready for them. Salmon are a big part of a bear's diet as they prepare to hibernate for the winter. You can see many exciting videos online showing bears' fishing skills as the salmon swim upstream. Because of the role salmon play in our ecosystem, hatcheries such as the Thornton Creek hatchery are critical to keeping the population of chinook healthy.

A bear enjoys a bite of salmon
Wikipedia: Image credit: Jennifer Allen.

QUALICUM BEACH MUSEUM

All photos courtesy of Qualicum Beach Museum

JUST THE FACTS

WHERE IS IT? 587 Beach Road, Qualicum Beach, BC, V9K 1K7;
(250) 752-5533
qbmuseum.ca

ARE PHOTOGRAPHS ALLOWED? Yes.

HOW DID IT START? What makes people want to start a museum? In 1983 Elizabeth Little and several friends thought it was important to celebrate the 100th anniversary of the first land title given in Qualicum Beach to a settler, Thomas Kincade. They created the Qualicum Beach Historical and Museum Society, which became official in 1984. The museum opened in 1988.

WHERE HAS IT LIVED?

The museum's first home was in a small power generating station that was once used to supply power to the town. The current main museum building was the original powerhouse of Port Alberni. The Qualicum Beach Historical and Museum Society bought the building in the early 1990s. After the building was **dismantled**, volunteers rebuilt it brick by brick where it lives today. This building opened to the public in 1995.

WHERE DO THE ITEMS COME FROM?

Items are donated to the museum from people who live in the area. Some items come from families of original settlers. They may not live in the area anymore, but when they are wondering what to do with historical items, they offer them to the museum for safekeeping.

HOW HAS IT CHANGED?

The archives and artifacts collections now live in the annex building, which was added in 2001. During recent renovations, the museum created the Graham Beard theatre, where you can see an amazing collection of fossils from Vancouver Island and around the world. A First Nations exhibit has been designed with help from Qualicum First Nation artist Jesse Recalma. Not all the treasures are inside. Outside, explore a mural painted on a storage shipping container by Indigenous artist Ocean Hyland and the restored totem pole crafted by Simon Charlie, master carver from the Cowichan Tribes of the Coast Salish Nation. Qualicum means "where the dog salmon run" in the Hul'qumi'num language. At the top of the pole a golden eagle holds a dog salmon in its talons. What other animals can you find?

See a 60,000-year-old walrus skull

ROSIE THE ICE AGE WALRUS

Rosie is a 60,000-year-old female walrus. Her scientific name is *Odobenus rosmarus*.

Bill Waterhouse, who was looking for shellfish on a very rocky beach near Qualicum Beach, found Rosie's jawbone in 1979.

When Bill's daughter saw the bone her father brought home, she thought her biology teacher, Graham Beard, would find it interesting, so she brought it to school the next day.

Her teacher immediately knew the bone was special and over a few weeks he carefully dug up the rest of the skeleton.

From 1999 to 2010, Rosie was on display at the Qualicum Beach Museum. She was then sent back to the Museum of Nature in Ottawa.

A visually impaired man, Don MacAlister, helped locate bones such as the **phalanges** and **metacarpals**. His sense of touch was so well developed he could find and identify these small bones.

Graham Beard agreed to ship Rosie's bones to the Museum of Nature in Ottawa. Experts put her bones together and, using **radiocarbon dating**, discovered her age.

Today a **resin replica** of Rosie's skull, as well as a genuine piece of her rib, is part of the Qualicum Beach Museum's **paleontology** display.

JADE ADZE BLADE

JUST THE FACTS

WHAT IS IT? This blade was part of an adze, used for carving wood.

WHAT DOES IT LOOK LIKE? The blade is made of nephrite, a type of jade. The tool has a bevelled edge. That means the edge is slanted. The blade was once attached to a handle. Depending on how the carver was using the blade, he could have used an elbow adze handle, which looks a little like an upper case J, or a d-adze handle, which is shaped like the letter D turned on its side.

WHERE DOES IT COME FROM? Although nephrite jade is not found on Vancouver Island, it was used by a number of First Nations People on the island. We know this because jade has been found locally by archeologists.

WHO USED IT? This type of tool was used by carvers for either canoe building or pole carving.

Tell Me More

Because jade is a tough mineral – meaning it doesn't break easily – it could be shaped into blades for carving tools. Jade can be found around Hope, BC, and toward the west coast of Washington state, so this jade may have come from there. Before European contact, Indigenous People had well-developed trading networks across North America. Wherever it came from, the carver who used this tool must have had something in their possession that they traded for the blade.

Different artists had different specialties. Some may have focused on large projects such as pole or canoe carving, while others carved smaller items like feast dishes or spindle whorls used for spinning.

Māori arrived in New Zealand in the 1300s, 300 years before European settlers. They came from the east Polynesian islands in boats or *waka* they carved from trees. Like coastal Indigenous Peoples, Māori used nephrite, or what they called *pounamu* blades like the one you see here, to hollow out trees for canoes. They carved beautiful designs on separate pieces of wood for the front (prow) and back (stern) of their canoes. These pieces could be removed when the canoe was not being used. They also used *pounamu* to make beautiful jewelry, as well as frightening weapons.

WHY IS THE JADE ADZE BLADE IMPORTANT IN THIS AREA?

Artists had special gifts and created beautiful carved objects. There were not always large numbers of artists in a community, which meant their skills were in high demand.

When this adze was made, money wasn't a sign of being rich. Instead, people would gather natural resources such as fish, as well as woven blankets, canoes and other **goods**. Then they'd give them all away at a Potlatch! The more you had to give away, the higher your status in the community. Families hosted Potlatches. Sometimes families would have a local artist create pieces for them. Other times they hired artists from other communities. These pieces were often special objects they wanted carved like masks and boxes and canoes. Because people had family ties in a number of different communities, they could reach out to other artists to help them create beautiful artworks to be used at their Potlatch.

A Maori war canoe, drawn in 1770 by Alexander Sporing
Source: Wikimedia Commons

JUST THE FACTS

WHAT IS IT? Hairdressers used the Branston Generator hairdressing tool to treat thinning hair, dandruff and even **eczema**. The hairdresser could also use this machine to provide soothing head massages.

WHAT DOES IT LOOK LIKE? Included in the box is a wand that looks a little like the handle of a curling iron. It plugs into a wall just like today's electronics. **Electrodes** (two can be seen here) attach to the handle. This is the "junior" model, which means it has fewer attachments than the full-sized model.

WHERE DOES IT COME FROM? Helen Eggersman owned the Branston Generator. She operated the first hairdressing salon in Qualicum Beach and donated her chair and many tools (including this one) to the museum.

WHO USED IT? Helen Eggersman used this tool.

BRANSTON GENERATOR HAIRDRESSING TOOL

Tell Me More

The company that made the Branston Generator claimed it could do amazing things, such as cure baldness and remove skin wrinkles. It is an example of false promises in advertising and the pressure both men and women feel to "fix" the natural way their bodies look. Although it looked pretty neat, the Branston Generator could not cure baldness or wrinkles – otherwise we'd still be using it today!

CONNECTIONS

In the 1920s, young women started cutting their hair. Before this, women wore their hair long in a **chignon** at the back of their necks, or in a bun on top of their heads. During the First World War, many women worked outside the home in factories. Long hair was often unsafe and short haircuts were not uncommon. After the war, short hair became a symbol of women's new independence, especially with young women. The "bob" was all the rage in the early and mid-'20s. Society was not accepting at first. Teachers, department store and office workers were often fired for having short hair. At first, many hairdressers didn't know how to create the short haircuts, so women went to barbers. Helen Eggersman wouldn't have had a problem, having been trained in both barbering and hairdressing. But by the time Helen was cutting hair, women were once again wearing their hair a little longer.

A newspaper article entitled "Bobbed Hair's the Thing!"
Source: Wikimedia Commons

⭐ WHY IS THE BRANSTON GENERATOR IMPORTANT IN THIS AREA?

Helen Eggersman was a brave and smart businesswoman. In 1929, at 16 years of age, she left Qualicum Beach to study hairdressing and barbering in Vancouver. When she was 18, she opened the first hair styling salon out of her home in Qualicum Beach. She started the salon when the Great Depression was just beginning. During the Depression, crops failed on the prairies, which meant farmers did not have produce to sell in Canada or to other countries. Many people lost money they had invested, lost their jobs and their homes. But Helen saw an opportunity in Qualicum Beach. People still needed to get their hair cut. She cut men's hair and cut and permed women's hair. Haircuts were one dollar and perms three dollars. The Branston Generator, which was the latest in hairdressing tools, shows how Helen was always on the "cutting edge" of her profession.

CUMBERLAND MUSEUM AND ARCHIVES

All photos courtesy of Cumberland Museum and Archives

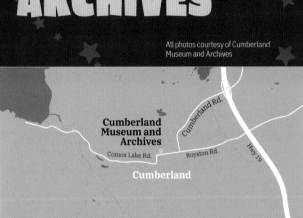

Cumberland Museum and Archives

Cumberland Rd.

Comox Lake Rd. Royston Rd. Hwy 19

Cumberland

JUST THE FACTS

WHERE IS IT? 2680 Dunsmuir Avenue, Cumberland, BC, V0R 1S0; (250) 336-2445
cumberlandmuseum.ca

ARE PHOTOGRAPHS ALLOWED? Yes.

HOW DID IT START? The Cumberland and District Historical Society started the museum and archives in 1981. This small community museum was supported by a large number of volunteers. They helped build the first exhibits, including the museum's mine experience you can still enjoy today. At the museum you'll learn the history of diverse groups of people who lived and worked in the area, and hear about people who influenced change and who came together to overcome challenges.

WHERE HAS IT LIVED?

The first museum started in 1969 and operated out of the printing office of the local newspaper, the *Cumberland Islander*. In 1980 the Village of Cumberland and the Cumberland and District Historical Society decided to construct a **purpose-built** museum for the community. The new Cumberland Museum and Archives opened in 1981 and has lived in its current location ever since.

WHERE DO THE ITEMS COME FROM?

The museum collects articles used in the community. Most often community members donate them. People who wish to donate an item fill in a form that the museum staff reviews to ensure the donor is the legal owner and that the story of the object fits with the museum's plan. Because each item tells a story, the museum staff wants to find out as much as possible about the item and how it is connected to the donor. Sometimes the museum receives something from another museum in a trade or transfer because that item is best suited to Cumberland's heritage.

HOW HAS IT CHANGED?

In 2020 the inside of the museum got a facelift. Not only has the building received a mechanical upgrade but there is also now more room for storing **archival materials** and **collection items**. The exhibits have also been refreshed and updated. In 2016 the Cumberland Museum and Archives became part of the Chinese Canadian Artifacts Project, hosted by the University of Victoria. You can go online and see artifacts and archival items from 16 different BC museums, showing the daily lives of Chinese Canadians from the late 1800s onward (https://ccap.uvic.ca/). The Cumberland museum has contributed over 1,200 **digitized** items to the project.

Learn how a baseball shirt tells a story about prejudice and injustice

ROYSTON BASEBALL JERSEY

This baseball jersey belonged to Shig Kiyono, a Japanese boy who played for the Royston Lumber baseball team in Cumberland. He left it behind when he was sent to an **internment camp** in 1942.

Baseball was a popular sport in the Japanese community in Cumberland. In 1914 the Japanese community built a baseball diamond.

Before the Second World War, there were at least five Japanese baseball teams in Cumberland: Royston Lumber, No. 5 Suns, No. 1 Nippons, Asama Stars and Cumberland Fujis. They competed in local tournaments around Vancouver Island.

Many Japanese Canadian boys who played in Cumberland dreamed of being **recruited** to Vancouver's **amateur** baseball team called the Vancouver Asahi.

The Asahi won many league championships, including five Pacific Northwest Championships in a row in the late 1930s. The team toured the United States and Japan. It was inducted into the Canadian Baseball Hall of Fame in 2003.

The Asahi players, who were often smaller than **Caucasian** players, invented what they called "brainball." They bunted, used **squeeze plays** and stole bases to help them win their games.

Online, you can watch *Heritage Minutes: Vancouver Asahi* (https://www.youtube.com/watch?v=wBv-MYAf9P0) and the National Film Board's documentary, *Sleeping Tigers: The Asahi Baseball Story* (https://www.nfb.ca/film/sleeping_tigers_the_asahi_baseball_story/).

Kenichi Doi, who played for Cumberland's Royston Lumber team, was recruited by the Vancouver Asahi in the 1920s. The Asahi team was forced to break up when Japanese Canadians were interned.

JUST THE FACTS

WHAT IS IT? It is a piano made by the Williams Piano Company.

WHAT DOES IT LOOK LIKE? This upright piano is 148 centimetres tall and 154 centimetres long. Are you taller or shorter than this piano?

WHERE DOES IT COME FROM? The piano was given to the museum in 1999, but no one knew who had donated it. When Sheila Heslop came to the museum to donate an article in 2019, she told museum staff she had also donated the piano. A 20-year-old mystery was solved.

WHO USED IT? Kay Finch, also known as Aunt Kay to those who lived in Cumberland, originally owned this piano. Many children learned how to play piano on this instrument.

LYDIA CATHERINE (KAY) FINCH'S PIANO

WOULD YOU BELIEVE?

All the keys of the piano's middle three **octaves** *are labelled. That's how we know beginners used this instrument. Kay Finch put the labels on the keys to help her young students learn the names of the notes.*

My Turn

What can you learn from the story of Kay Finch and her piano?

CONNECTIONS

Music is something that every culture creates. Chinese music and musical instruments go back thousands of years. They played chimes, bells, flutes, drums and stringed instruments. But before the 1600s keyboard instruments did not exist in China. A clavichord – an instrument that looks a little like the modern piano – was brought to China by a missionary. Pianos became popular with the emperors. **Missionaries** brought pianos and organs with them to play in their churches. By the early 1900s, learning to play the piano was an important part of a good education. Chinese Canadian parents in Cumberland must have been very happy that Aunt Kay taught piano. Some say she never made her students pay for the lessons.

⭐ WHY IS THE PIANO IMPORTANT IN THIS AREA?

Kay Finch was a loved and respected member of the Cumberland community. Kay taught Sunday school at the Anglican (Chinese) **mission**. She also taught piano, English, **needle arts** and painting to many Chinese Canadian children. Today we would not think this was unusual, but back then it was. At the beginning of the 20th century, Chinese Canadians were not always treated well. By 1903 the Canadian government charged a "head tax" of $500.00 to every Chinese person who wanted to come to Canada. In Cumberland many Chinese men worked in the mines. There were many **prejudices** in those days, so some members of the community may have looked down upon Kay's behaviour.

A Happy Birthdau celebration for Mrs. Finch

Tell Me More

The piano was built sometime between 1902 and 1904 in Oshawa, Ontario. This model, the New Scale, was one of the best Williams pianos a person could buy in those days. At that time it took from ten weeks to three months to make one piano. Williams pianos were not just well known in Canada. They were shipped to several countries around the world, including Australia and New Zealand. We don't know exactly when Kay bought the piano, or whether it was new or used, but we do know she sold it to Sheila Heslop in 1969 for $50.00.

JUST THE FACTS

UNION PIN

WHAT IS IT? This pin shows that the wearer paid money to support people who were part of a large strike in Winnipeg in 1919.

WHAT DOES IT LOOK LIKE? The large letters say, "Labor's Liberty Bond." A bond is a little like paper money. It has a dollar amount printed on it. The difference is you can't spend it right away. It is only worth the amount printed on it after a certain number of years.

WHERE DOES IT COME FROM? Norah Davis donated the pin in 1993.

WHO USED IT? This pin belonged to Joe Naylor, an important person in the **union movement**. A union is made up of workers who have the same type of job. They could be miners, loggers, firefighters – even teachers. They form a union to stand together and to make sure their members are treated fairly.

Tell Me More

In 1919, in Winnipeg, workers from many different types of work went on strike. That means they did not go in to work. About 30,000 people walked off their jobs. The population of Winnipeg was 200,000 people at the time, so 30,000 people on strike is very big! At the end of the six-week strike, many of the leaders were arrested. The money made from the Labor's Liberty Bond you see on the pin helped pay for the lawyers. Even though Joe Naylor lived in BC, he supported the Winnipeg workers.

WOULD YOU BELIEVE?

Because Joe helped organize Vancouver Island's coal miners' strike, which lasted from 1912 to 1914, he was **blacklisted**. *That means no one would hire him. He was unemployed for ten years.*

My Turn

In the early 1900s, Chinese and Japanese workers were not allowed to join the miners union. What reasons can you think of for letting all workers into the union?

CONNECTIONS

Pins are still used today. During elections people often wear pins to show who they are voting for. People will also wear pins to protest against something that is happening in their community or in their country. During the COVID-19 pandemic, hospital workers had to wear masks and face shields to keep healthy. In at least two hospitals they made buttons with their pictures on them so patients would know what they looked like.

WHY IS THE PIN IMPORTANT IN THIS AREA?

In the early 20th century, Joe Naylor helped organize unions, especially for miners. Mining was a dangerous job and Joe wanted to make sure mine owners followed rules that would keep their workers safe. Mine owners often brought people in from China and Japan but didn't pay them as well as the white workers. Joe thought there should be a minimum wage for all workers. He believed in fair treatment for everyone. That's probably one reason he bought a Labor's Liberty Bond – to help out the Winnipeg strikers.

MUSEUM AT CAMPBELL RIVER

Photo: Courtesy of the Museum at Campbell River

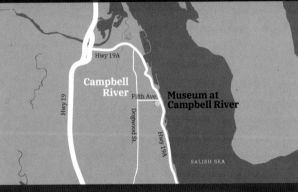

JUST THE FACTS

WHERE IS IT? 470 Island Highway at 5th Avenue, Campbell River, BC, V9W 4Z9; (250) 287-3103
crmuseum.ca

ARE PHOTOGRAPHS ALLOWED? Photos are allowed in some parts of the museum, but not in others. Watch for signs that will tell you where they are allowed.

HOW DID IT START? In 1958 a group of people interested in the history of northern Vancouver Island and in Indigenous art and culture got together to create a society that would eventually oversee the museum.

WHERE HAS IT LIVED?

There wasn't a museum when the first exhibit was displayed in the lobby of a sports fishing lodge. The first museum shared space with the library in the basement of the municipal hall then moved with the library to a new location constructed for Canada's centennial. The current building opened in 1994.

WHERE DO THE ITEMS COME FROM?

Many items are donated. But there are other ways objects come to the museum. Some personal belongings are on long-term loan or are loaned to the museum so they can be stored safely. When objects are found during an **archeological investigation** in the area (from about 25 kilometres south of Campbell River to as far north as Bella Bella), the museum will hold and preserve the items in trust for the people of British Columbia, especially the Indigenous People who are associated with the objects.

HOW HAS IT CHANGED?

The new building is the biggest change in the museum's history. Although the building was finished in 1994, there were no permanent exhibits! It took until around 2006 to complete the space with all the beautiful items you see today. Experts on the history of the area and the customs and culture of those who have lived on the land for thousands of years and those who settled here more recently helped develop topics that could be covered in the exhibits. Staff and volunteers raised money and worked on finding items and building structures for displays. Today you can see permanent exhibitions, as well as temporary and travelling exhibits.

CANNERY TOKENS

Photo: Courtesy of the Museum at Campbell River

William Edward Anderson owned Quathiaski Cannery from 1908 to 1938. In the early years of the cannery, he did not pay his fishermen with money. He paid them with these tokens.

When Anderson was selling the cannery, he asked Billy Assu, Harry Assu, Johnny Dick and Jimmy Hovel – all We Wai Kai fishermen – to choose from three companies that were bidding for the cannery. They chose BC Packers.

...e number on the coin was the ...ber of fish the fisherman caught. ...e tokens ranged from 1 to 100.

On these aluminum tokens, you can read the words "Not Transferable." That means the tokens could not be traded for real money.

Anderson started to track the number of fish caught by each man in a book. Men could withdraw money based on the number of fish they caught, but they didn't have to take the whole amount owed to them.

...n tokens couldn't be spent like ...ular currency. Tommy Hall, a ...dra Island fisherman, said, ...h tokens...couldn't get you to a ...ce you wanted to go to."

Anderson stopped using the tokens in 1917. Chief Billy Assu and the other **We Wai Kai fishermen** convinced him to change the system.

The only place these coins could be used was at Quathiaski Cannery's general store. Making the fishermen use the company store kept them in debt to the cannery owner.

W. E. ANDERSON
QUATHIASKI
COVE.
B. C.

JUST THE FACTS

WHAT IS IT? This pole was carved for the museum based on an original 1960s pole designed and carved by Sam Henderson.

WHAT DOES IT LOOK LIKE? The pole is really tall – over 6.5 metres. If your bed is around 190 centimetres, how many beds tall is this pole? The pole is carved and painted. The Thunderbird, a Supernatural creature with its yellow beak and legs and wings outstretched, sits above a brown bear holding a small man.

WHERE DOES IT COME FROM? The Thunderbird Bear Pole was carved by Sam Henderson's son, Bill, and his grandsons, Junior and Greg.

WHO USED IT? The museum is lucky enough to have this beautiful pole in a protected place on the property.

Tell Me More

The original pole carved by Sam was commissioned by the Department of Highways for a project celebrating Canada's 100th birthday. The pole was raised in front of the first purpose-built home of the museum, which was also built to celebrate Canada's centennial. When the museum moved to its current home, the pole was left behind. Eight years later, the pole was restored by Sam's son, Bill, and moved to the museum's grounds.

THUNDERBIRD BEAR POLE

Bill Henderson at the Thunder Bird Bear Pole blessing.
Photo: Courtesy of the Museum at Campbell River

CONNECTIONS

The Thunderbird and the bear crests on both the museum's pole and the original pole belong to May Quocksister's family. May was Sam Henderson's wife and Bill's mother. The Quocksister/Kwawkseestahla family has a deep history in Campbell River. Find the story of the *piika-uu*, in the Alberni Valley Museum. The images woven into these baskets are also passed down through many generations.

My Turn

Bill Henderson was inspired to take up carving by his father. Is there someone in your life who has inspired you to take up a skill like playing a musical instrument, painting, Lego building, knitting or fixing cars? You can see Bill's story, *Learning from the Master: The Legacy of Sam Henderson*, on the Museum at Campbell River's YouTube page.

★ WHY IS THE THUNDERBIRD BEAR POLE IMPORTANT IN THIS AREA?

On the museum grounds, the original pole overlooked Discovery Passage. It was battered by wind, rain and snow and, over time, the wood became spongy. It couldn't be restored again. In April 2016, Bill requested the pole be taken down so he could ceremonially burn it on the Campbell River Spit. Bill said, "I laid out my father's favourite foods on top of the pole before it was burned: tea and crackers and smoked fish and herring roe. Then we blessed the new log at the same time. To me in my heart, that was the best thing to do." Bill and his nephew Junior started carving the new pole. It has the same **crests** and painting style as the original pole. When the new pole was raised, the Henderson family blessed it. This pole shows the long relationship between the museum and the Henderson family.

Photo: Courtesy of the Museum at Campbell River

JUST THE FACTS

WHAT IS IT? The *Soyokaze* (which means "Gentle Wind" in Japanese) is a restored, 11-metre-long, cod fishing boat.

WHAT DOES IT LOOK LIKE? It is a double-ended boat (meaning the front and back are both pointed) made from cedar planking. The engine room is located in the front (bow) and the living quarters in the back (stern).

WHERE DOES IT COME FROM? Shigekazu "Smiley" Matsunaga owned the boat. He donated it to the museum. The museum staff and specialists restored the boat.

WHO USED IT? Mr. Matsunaga had this boat made by the Kishi Boatworks in 1939. He fished with this boat until it was taken from him by the Canadian government after Pearl Harbor was bombed on December 7, 1941.

Photo: Courtesy of the Museum at Campbell River

The Middle
› MUSEUM AT CAMPBELL RIVER

THE SOYOKAZE

Tell Me More

Mr. Matsunaga was born in Canada, educated in Japan and returned to Quathiaski Cove on Quadra Island. He helped his uncle fish for lingcod then set up own fishing business. Because of the fishing and canning industry, Quathiaski Cov was a multicultural community. Indigenous People, along with people of Chinese, Japanese and European ancestry, all lived and worked in the area. When Pearl Ha was bombed in 1941, the Canadian government took away Japanese Canadian fishermen's boats but promised to hold them in trust. The boats were then adverti for sale. If the fishermen didn't agree to the price offered to them (which was alwa below what the boats were worth), their boats were sold without their **consent**.

WOULD YOU BELIEVE?

The Soyokaze *may be the only* confiscated *boat that was ever reclaimed by the Japanese Canadian family that originally owned it.*

My Turn

Why do you think the story of the *Soyokaze* is an important story for Canadians to learn about?

CONNECTIONS

In 2011 a Japanese fisherman, Kou Sasaki, lost his boat in a tsunami that devastated the town of Ofunato, Japan. In 2013 a boat washed up on the northwest coast of BC and was towed to Klemtu. The manager of the Spirit Bear Lodge in Klemtu asked one of his guests, Ms. Yoshi Karasawa, if she could help find the owner. The boat had Japanese writing and Ms. Karasawa recognized it as a Japanese fishing boat. It had drifted almost 7000 kilometres across the ocean, its Yamaha motor still attached. With help from her friend, and assistant curator at the West Vancouver Museum, Ms. Karasawa was able to find the owner. Mr. Sasaki told her he had owned the *Somatsumaru* (Twin Pines) since 1985 and it was like his child. He didn't want the boat back, but the Kitasoo First Nation offered to host him as their guest in Klemtu so he could see his boat once again.

⭐ WHY IS THE SOYOKAZE IMPORTANT IN THIS AREA?

During the Japanese Canadian Internment, Japanese Canadian families were uprooted and sent to camps away from the coast during the Second World War. Very few came back to their hometowns after the war. But the Matsunagas did. And they started fishing again. Because the *Soyokaze* had been sold by the government, Mr. Matsunaga had to buy different boats, but he never stopped looking for the *Soyokaze*. In 1957 another fisherman reported that he had seen Mr. Matsunaga's boat, but it had a new name, *North Star II*. Mr. Matsunaga was able to buy back his boat because the people who had it realized he was the original owner.

Mr. Matsunaga never changed the name of the boat back to the *Soyokaze*. He fished from that boat until 1980. He felt his boat was an important part of Canada's and Quadra Island's history and he hoped the museum would want it. Today the *Soyokaze* sits at the entrance to the museum.

Some of the devastation left by the tsunami that hit Ofunato in 2011.

JUST THE FACTS

WHAT IS IT? This cedar sculpture represents a Thunderbird.

WHAT DOES IT LOOK LIKE? The Thunderbird's massive, outstretched wings span 3.7 metres. That's about one and a half times the length of a queen-size bed. It's as tall as the average professional basketball player. With a hooked beak and horns on its head, the Thunderbird looks all-powerful.

WHERE DOES IT COME FROM? The Thunderbird stood in the cemetery on the Campbell River Spit, marking the grave of Tsok-sa-yaids Kwawkseestahla (**anglicized** to Tom Quocksister) who died in 1905. However, it was originally carved much earlier, in the 1800s, for his grandfather.

WHO USED IT? The Kwawkseestahla family used it as a grave marker.

Tell Me More

Starting in the late 19th century, Indigenous children were taken from their families and put into residential schools. Indigenous Peoples and their cultures were under attack by the Canadian government. During this time, collectors from around the world rushed in to snap up Indigenous belongings. In 1912, following a concerted campaign by Fred Nunns, the Kwawkseestahla family **reluctantly** sold the Thunderbird. It was taken from the cemetery and put into the provincial museum in Victoria. It was far away from the Kwawkseestahla family, and they hoped to bring it back to its home.

KWAWKSEESTAHLA/ QUOCKSISTER THUNDERBIRD

Photo: Courtesy of the Museum at Campbell Riv

The famous Canadian artist Emily Carr sketched and then painted this Thunderbird in 1912 when it was still in the cemetery. You can look up her painting, Graveyard Entrance, Campbell River, on the internet. How does the museum's picture of the Thunderbird differ from the painting?

Look at the pages for the Thunderbird Bear Pole. The original pole was carved by Sam Henderson. Before Sam carved this pole, he carved a replica of the Kwawkseestahla/Quocksister Thunderbird for the Museum at Campbell River. Sam was married to May Quocksister and had been adopted into her family, so recreating this monument was a natural fit. The Thunderbird was his first monumental carving. Sam's replica is now in storage but has been displayed many times as an example of his early large-scale work.

My Turn

What questions do you have about the Kwawkseestahla/Quocksister Thunderbird? Write a letter or email to the Museum at Campbell River and see what answers you get in return.

⭐ WHY IS THE KWAWKSEESTAHLA/QUOCKSISTER THUNDERBIRD IMPORTANT IN THIS AREA?

In 2005 the Kwawkseestahla family came to an agreement with the Royal BC Museum and the Museum at Campbell River for the sculpture to return to Campbell River. After the family gathered at the cemetery and welcomed the Thunderbird home, it was taken to the museum where it proudly stands at the entrance to the exhibits.

This Thunderbird is one of very few items in the community today that dates back to a time before the **Potlatch ban**, when Indigenous People were able to practise their culture freely. Many Indigenous artifacts were burned, or they were taken away and put into museums around the world.

The collectors assumed that Indigenous People and their culture would be stamped out or **assimilated**. They were wrong. Indigenous People are strong and resilient, and even though they suffered under government attacks, their cultures continue and **flourish** today.

JUST THE FACTS

FLOATHOUSE

WHAT IS IT? As the name suggests, this is a house that can float on water.

WHAT DOES IT LOOK LIKE? The one room in this compact house served as a living and dining area, kitchen and bedroom. The house was built on floats so a tugboat could tow it from logging camp to logging camp.

WHERE DOES IT COME FROM? This floathouse was made especially for the museum based on August Schnarr's floathouse. Many different people donated the items in the house.

WHO USED IT? Families of trappers and **hand loggers** used floathouses. Between the 1890s and the 1940s, logging companies moved along the coast cutting trees. There were few beaches or other flat areas where camps could be built, so floathouses worked well. Loggers who lived in these houses could move with the company.

Photo: Courtesy of the
Museum at Campbell River

Tell Me More

Although this house looks cozy, living in a floathouse was difficult. Winters were cold. The house was insulated with newspapers, and a wood stove was the only source of heat. Kids didn't have rooms to go to when they wanted to get away from their parents or their brothers and sisters. Life jackets were part of every kid's wardrobe and were worn from morning to night. Logger and trapper August Schnarr, who lived on a floathouse like this, had three daughters. When his wife died, the girls were often left for several weeks at a time while he trapped. In the 1930s, they had two pet cougars. Imagine what that must have been like!

CONNECTIONS

Early settlers knew the insulating quality of newspapers and that's why floathouses had newspapers attached to their walls. Still, the way the papers were used didn't keep the floathouses too warm. Today newspapers are made into ecofriendly, highly effective insulation – but not by pasting them on the walls. They are shredded into tiny pieces and mixed with boric acid. The acid helps to make the insulation fire-safe and resistant to pests and mold. When the insulation has passed fire testing, it is packaged and sold. A professional installer sprays the insulation into spaces between walls and between rafters in the attic. What a great way to reuse and recycle newspapers.

My Turn

Make a list of advantages and disadvantages of growing up on a floathouse in the 1930s. Think about your parents or guardians, as well as you and any brothers or sisters you might have. Based on your list and considering your personality, explain why you would or wouldn't have liked to live on a floathouse back then.

★ WHY IS THE FLOATHOUSE IMPORTANT IN THIS AREA?

The women who lived on these floathouses had to be courageous and resilient. Their husbands were away for several days in a row and they were responsible for all the household duties, plus raising children. If there was no school, students took correspondence courses. But, remember, there were no computers in those days. They sent their assignments to the teacher by mail. Women had to know first aid and herbal remedies for coughs and colds. Once a week, the union steamship arrived with mail and goods. Families also depended on the Columbia Coast Mission boat (run by the Anglican Church). It had a floating hospital, movie theatre and library. Visiting nurses gave vaccinations. To overcome loneliness, women created clubs and sports teams, sewing classes and social events. Going to an event often meant a risky boat ride to a community far away.

JUST THE FACTS

DZUNUK̓WA FEAST DISH

WHAT IS IT? This dramatic dish would have been used for serving large amounts of food at Potlatches.

WHAT DOES IT LOOK LIKE? The feast dish is 300 centimetres tall if it's standing on its end. How tall are you? The dish is in the shape of Dzunuk'wa, a female giant of the woods who carries a basket on her back into which she puts children who have wandered away.

WHERE DOES IT COME FROM? This dish was carved in the 1800s for the Smith family. They used it at Potlatches. Eventually, they put it on display in front of their Big House on Campbell River Spit. Liǧʷiɫdax̌ʷ (Lekwiltok) Chief Charles Smith gave the dish to Herbert and Dolly Pidcock around 1924. They donated it to the museum in 1959.

WHO USED IT? The Smith family used it for Potlatches and later for display.

Tell Me More

This feast dish holds many secrets. During a Potlatch, Chief Charles Smith would have served food to hundreds of people. The giant's belly might have been filled with delicious seafood. Perched on the giant's knees would have been smaller dishes of other scrumptious food. Hidden behind the face is another bowl. The hot food in that bowl would make steam rise from the eyes and mouth of Dzunuk 'wa. Imagine seeing the woman giant belching smoke!

Photo: Courtesy of the Museum at Campbell River

Colonization happens when a country takes control of lands outside its borders and turns those lands into a colony. Britain, France, Belgium, the Netherlands, Denmark, Portugal and Spain, to name a few, had colonies outside their borders. Both France and England colonized Canada. What often happens during colonization is the colonizers remove precious cultural objects from the countries they have taken over. For example, because Africa was colonized by many European nations, thousands of African artifacts are in museums around the world. For many of these artifacts, there is no proof that the objects were given willingly or with consent. There are at least 90,000 African items in French museums alone. Around the world there are discussions about whether or not museums should return items that were taken without permission and, if they do, how it should be done.

My Turn

Belongings associated with the Potlatch are important to the identity of many coastal First Nations. These belongings tell who each family is and what rights and privileges belong to that family. What objects do you or your family have that tell who you are? How would you feel if those objects were taken away from you?

WHY IS THE FEAST DISH IMPORTANT IN THIS AREA?

A family hosts a Potlatch on special occasions like naming a child, celebrating a marriage and mourning a death. "Potlatch" means "to give." At a potlatch in the 1900s, the host gave away gifts like copper bracelets, carvings and **oolichan oil** (T'lina). Today oolichan oil is still given, as well as silver jewelry and household items like homemade preserves and knitted and crocheted dishcloths. There is singing and dancing and lots of food. From 1885 until 1951, Potlatches were illegal. If people were caught holding or attending a Potlatch, they were charged by police. Then they were given a choice: turn over their cultural objects like masks and bentwood boxes, or face going to jail. **Indian Agents** often sold **surrendered** items to museums around the world. After many hard-fought battles by Indigenous People, some – but not all – belongings taken from them have been given back or **repatriated**.

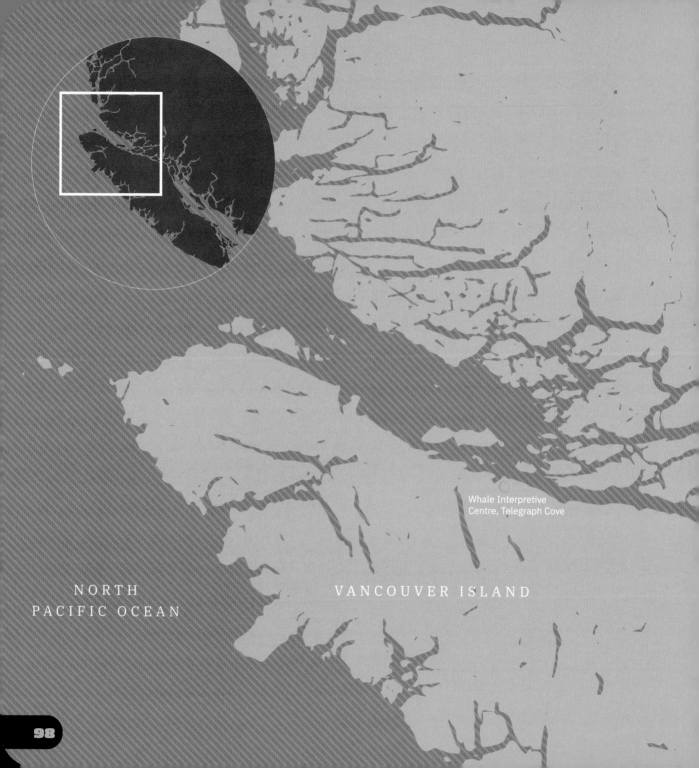

NORTH
PACIFIC OCEAN

VANCOUVER ISLAND

Whale Interpretive
Centre, Telegraph Cove

THE NORTH

THE WHALE INTERPRETIVE CENTRE

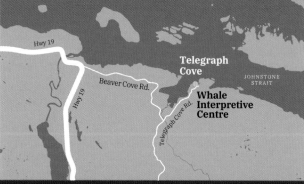

JUST THE FACTS

WHERE IS IT? Telegraph Cove, BC, V0N 3J0; (250) 928-3129 (May–September 30 only)
killerwhalecentre.org

ARE PHOTOGRAPHS ALLOWED? Yes.

HOW DID IT START? A committee co-chaired by the late Dr. Michael Bigg led to the creation of the Johnstone Strait Killer Whale Interpretive Centre Society. It was incorporated in the early 1990s. The Whale Interpretive Centre (WIC) opened its doors in 2002.

All photos are courtesy of the Whale Interpretive Centre.

WHERE HAS IT LIVED?

The WIC hasn't moved from the old **freight shed** where it started, but the building has been completely rebuilt.

WHERE DO THE ITEMS COME FROM?

All of the skeletons come from marine mammals that have died in accidents or from natural causes. No marine mammals are killed for the museum.

HOW HAS IT CHANGED?

The collection has grown over the years as the museum has found or been given more species. An adult Bigg's killer whale arrived in May 2018. Its **articulated** bones were suspended from the ceiling of the museum.

Inside the Interpretive centre

Learn about a sea lion from its bones

STELLER SEA LION

Steller sea lions belong to the pinniped group of mammals. Pinniped means "wing or fin-footed." These sea lions have four wing-like flippers. On land they can walk on their flippers. In the water they pull themselves with their front flippers.

The average male is about three metres long and weighs about 700 kilograms. But they can get as heavy as 1100 kilograms. Females are smaller and weigh about half as much.

Steller sea lions live on the west coast of British Columbia. They eat fish, squid and octopus.

Although Steller sea lions have flippers, the bones of the flippers look similar to human hands. How are they alike? How are they different?

A male sea lion is called a bull, a female is called a cow and a baby is called a pup.

Steller sea lions make a growling sound.

Steller sea lions are the largest sea lion on Earth.

The Bigg's killer whale is the Steller sea lion's main **predator**.

The Steller sea lion you see at the WIC was found near Telegraph Cove and was articulated, or put back together, by volunteers and centre staff.

NORTHERN RESIDENT KILLER WHALE

JUST THE FACTS

WHAT IS IT? The northern resident killer whale is a fish-eating orca or killer whale.

WHAT DOES IT LOOK LIKE? The northern resident killer whale you see at the WIC is a juvenile, meaning it was not a baby but was still quite young when it died.

WHERE DOES IT COME FROM? This killer whale was found near Namu, on the central coast of BC.

WHO USED IT? Like all the animals at the WIC, the skeleton of this northern resident killer whale (orca) is used to teach visitors about the different types of whales that visit Johnstone Strait, Blackfish Sound and the Broughton **Archipelago** area.

WOULD YOU BELIEVE?

The words "orca" and "whale" cannot be used together. You can talk about an orca or a killer whale, but never an orca whale.

My Turn

What could a young person your age do to help the resident killer whales?

Tell Me More

The northern resident population of orcas communicates with sound. There are three sound clans within this population. The sounds in each clan are very different from one another, but all of the orcas within a particular clan share several identical calls. Within each sound clan there are mother-led groups (**matrilines**) that all share the same sounds. At the WIC you can hear the languages of each of the three clans.

CONNECTIONS

There are two different populations of resident killer whales: the northern resident killer whale, and the southern resident killer whale. They might have similar names, but they are two different populations. Southern resident killer whales are on the endangered species list. Underwater noise from large ships makes it hard for these orcas to use **echolocation** to find food. Water pollution affects the quality and the quantity of the food they eat. In 2020 there were only 74 southern resident killer whales in our ocean.

⭐ WHY IS THE NORTHERN RESIDENT KILLER WHALE IMPORTANT IN THIS AREA?

In 2001 northern resident killer whales were considered threatened by the Canadian government. The areas near Telegraph Cove, BC, have been identified as **critical habitat** but are not yet protected by the federal government.

The northern resident population gathers in this area during many times of the year, because when salmon are migrating back to the rivers in which they were born, they swim through Johnstone Strait. Salmon are a major food source for northern resident killer whales.

JUST THE FACTS

› THE WHALE INTERPRETIVE CENTRE

T44 BIGG'S KILLER WHALE

WHAT IS IT? This skeleton is a Bigg's killer whale, a marine mammal-eating killer whale.

WHAT DOES IT LOOK LIKE? Scientists have been photo-identifying and counting killer whales since the 1970s. They discovered early on that not all killer whales looked the same. Dr. Michael Bigg realized there were scratches on the saddle patch (white area behind the **dorsal fin**) and marks and **notches** on dorsal fins that were like fingerprints – each one completely different. T44 had a notch on the back edge of its dorsal fin, as well as some scratches on its saddle patch.

WHERE DOES IT COME FROM? The Coast Guard vessel, *Provo Wallace*, found T44 north of Port Hardy in 2009.

WHO USED IT? The WIC uses the skeleton to teach visitors about this amazing marine mammal.

Tell Me More

Bringing a dead whale back to Telegraph Cove is always hard, and T44 was no different. It took two days of towing before the whale arrived safely. To try to find out why a whale has died, scientists do a **necropsy**. Scientists and volunteers conducted the necropsy on T44.

It took eight years to clean the whale and to raise enough money to have the whale articulated. An articulator is a person who puts the bones back together. Some bones were missing, so a team from the University of Victoria 3D printed what was needed to complete the skeleton. The final step was hanging the skeleton at the WIC, where T44 seems to be swimming above you.

WOULD YOU BELIEVE?

T44's stomach contents included over 300 seal claws (that's about 15 harbour seals) and broken teeth from dolphins and porpoises. Two flipper tags told scientists that the whale had also eaten two juvenile elephant seals born at a rookery in Northern California!

My Turn

What do you think you can learn by looking at an animal's skeleton?

CONNECTIONS

Saddle patches and dorsal fins help researchers recognize individual killer whales. But how do you identify something like a grizzly bear? In 2020 a **behavioural ecologist** and two software designers worked on facial recognition software to help identify grizzlies. It's not easy. The team needs lots of pictures of different bears so the software can learn which bear is which. Unlike humans, bears don't sit still to have their photos taken. And it's harder to get close to a grizzly than it is to get close to a killer whale. Researchers put cameras in the areas where the bears live and hope the pictures will give them clear images of the bears' faces.

⭐ WHY IS THE BIGG'S KILLER WHALE IMPORTANT IN THIS AREA?

Dr. Bigg noticed that some killer whales visiting his study areas were not associating with the resident killer whales. He realized they were a completely different population. They made different sounds and had some obvious differences in their physical appearance. This group of whales is now called Bigg's killer whales.

The Bigg's killer whale is at the top of the food chain. It eats other marine mammals such as dolphins, porpoises, sea lions, seals and even other types of whales. A healthy Bigg's killer whale population keeps the numbers of other marine mammals from growing too large and unbalancing the ocean's ecosystem. Under Canada's Federal Species at Risk Act, Bigg's killer whales are threatened. The population of these killer whales has been increasing for several decades and in 2020 was approximately 350.

Sea lions are food for the Bigg's killer whale.

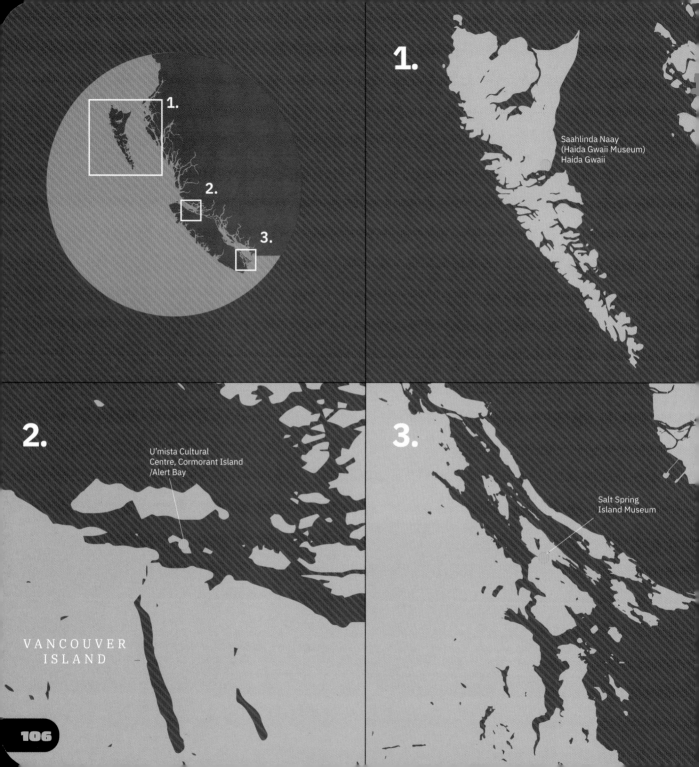

1.

Saahlinda Naay
(Haida Gwaii Museum)
Haida Gwaii

2.

U'mista Cultural
Centre, Cormorant Island
/Alert Bay

VANCOUVER
ISLAND

3.

Salt Spring
Island Museum

THE ISLANDS

SALT SPRING MUSEUM

WHERE HAS IT LIVED?

Bittancourt House, where the museum is housed, was donated to the Salt Spring Farmers' Institute. The historic house was built in 1884 as a dowry house. Traditionally, a dowry is a gift like jewelry, money or property given to the groom by the bride's family on their marriage. The idea is that this gift will help set up the family home. Bittancourt House was originally built as a dowry for one of the family's daughters. Estalon Bittancourt and his wife, Mary Katherine, had five boys and six girls.

The house was moved from Estalon Bittancourt's property at Vesuvius Bay to land owned by the Farmers' Institute on Rainbow Road in 1980. The museum's purpose is to talk about the early settlers who came to the island.

WHERE DO THE ITEMS COME FROM?

The museum is made up of local artifacts donated or loaned by local families.

HOW HAS IT CHANGED?

Over the years, to keep up with the museum's expanding collection, volunteers from the Farmers' Institute have constructed three additions expanding the museum from four rooms to seven. These days the museum has a collection spanning from the 1880s to the 1950s.

JUST THE FACTS

WHERE IS IT? Farmers' Institute 351 Rainbow Road, Salt Spring Island, BC, V8K 2M4; (250) 537-4895
saltspringmuseum.com

ARE PHOTOGRAPHS ALLOWED? Yes

HOW DID IT START? The museum opened in 1978. The Salt Spring Farmers' Institute started it. Founded in 1895, the institute works to help farmers and their interests. Today the museum is run by its sister organization, the Salt Spring Farmers' Heritage Foundation. It's a group that is dedicated to promoting agriculture education, with projects like the museum.

In a museum you can:

imagine what it was like to live on an island

INSULATED CONTAINER

This insulated container was used to ship ice cream to Salt Spring Island before they had refrigerators on the island. The insulated container is from the Superior Ice Cream Company.

When the ice cream was delivered off the ship, the padded containers had a package of dry ice on top of the ice cream below the top flap of the container. Occasionally, one of the kids would get to hold one of the packages. They liked to drop them off the wharf into the water to watch all the bubbles coming up. It was like watching a carbonated drink being poured from a glass.

Dry ice is a solid form of carbon dioxide, a gas that is released into the air by all animals when they breathe out.

It arrived at the dock on the south end of the island. Children would be lined up waiting for its arrival. Would you have lined up for ice cream?

The flavours were limited. There was vanilla and strawberry, and probably chocolate. Mouats' store in Ganges, which sold the ice cream, couldn't accommodate too many containers at a time.

Electricity didn't come to Salt Spring until 1937. The Mouats operated their own generator. Houses didn't have refrigerators, let alone ones with a freezer compartment.

Nowadays BC Ferries is one of the largest ferry systems in the world. It moves about 60,000 people a day throughout coastal BC. That's like moving the entire population of Port Coquitlam, BC, somewhere every day.

JUST THE FACTS

WHAT IS IT? A delivery boat that was part of a **fleet** used to ship farm and market garden produce from Salt Spring Island to Vancouver Island for local markets.

WHAT DOES IT LOOK LIKE? It's a long, white, narrow boat called a clinker.

WHERE DOES IT COME FROM? The family of William MacDonald of Salt Spring Island donated the boat. The museum doesn't know who the original owner was.

WHO USED IT? Many of the Japanese immigrants to the island were market gardeners and were dependent on this service to get their produce to a larger market. Japanese immigrants started arriving on the island around 1896. They had a reputation for being hard working, often working on farms and homesteads belonging to white settlers. By the time the Second World War broke out, there was a close-knit group of 77 Japanese Canadians living on Salt Spring, known for their generosity and community spirit.

DELIVERY BOAT

Tell Me More

The Okanos family started out making their living by fishing, but by 1924 the had begun farming. They sold their strawberries, raspberries and vegetables to a produce distributor in Victoria. During the 1930s, when things were hard because of the Great Depression, the Okanos family helped out their neighbours who were starving by giving them chickens and eggs.

Their daughter, Kimiko Murakami, and her husband, Katsuyori Murakami, who farmed close by, grew strawberries and asparagus. They supplied produce to the Empress Hotel in Victoria. In addition, they kept chickens and sold the eggs. Kimik was the first woman driver on Salt Spring. She'd used her parents' Model T truck t deliver eggs to the store in Ganges.

My Turn

Check out the National Film Board's film *Minoru: Memory of Exile*, by Japanese Canadian Michael Fukushima. It tells the story of his Canadian-born father's childhood during the internment and moving back to Japan.

CONNECTIONS

Damnoen Saduak is one of the oldest floating markets in Bangkok, Thailand. A popular tourist destination, it draws people from around the world for the opportunity to experience the chaos and colour. From their wooden boats called sampans, female vendors, dressed in blue fabric shirts called Mo Hom and straw hats, sell tasty treats like Pad Thai, dragon ball and mangoes as well as bright textile art and hats.

Though these days the market is very touristy, it shares an important connection to the city's past. In the 19th century, when the city became known as the Venice of the East, the focus of life was the city's waterways and canals. Back then, boats were the most popular form of transportation and the waterways linked people to their houses and temples, as well as providing space for commercial markets.

⭐ WHY IS THE DELIVERY BOAT IMPORTANT IN THIS AREA?

Japanese Canadians played a large role in the history of the island, but few people know this. In 1939, during the lead-up to the Second World War, the Canadian government mistreated this community. It feared these citizens would collaborate with its enemy, Japan. This distrust led it to forcibly move Japanese Canadians to internment camps in the interior of BC and other provinces. After the war, the federal government made it impossible for them to return to their former lives by forbidding it.

During the war, government agents took everything away from them without their consent. This was made possible by the **War Measures Act**. They lost everything, including their houses and property, things they had worked a lifetime to earn, as well as special heirlooms that might have been in their family for many years.

JUST THE FACTS

> SALT SPRING MUSEUM

WILLIS'S RELOADER

WHAT IS IT? An antique tool for reloading rifle cartridges.

WHAT DOES IT LOOK LIKE? It's green and looks like a strange combination of a screwdriver and a handheld mixer.

WHERE DOES IT COME FROM? This tool belonged to Willis Stark, a Black settler on Salt Spring Island. His mother, Sylvia, was one of the first non-Indigenous women to ever visit Salt Spring Island. Things were hard for Willis's parents and siblings when they first arrived. There were risks: wild animals, diseases, injuries.

WHO USED IT? Willis used it. He was a respected hunter who was called on when there was a problem with cougars. These predators were a big problem on the island, often attacking farmers' livestock. He also made money hunting deer, pheasant and grouse. He could make as much as $10 for a deer's carcass.

Tell Me More

Despite having a successful farm, the Stark family moved to the Nanaimo area on Vancouver Island. After two years, Sylvia and Willis moved back to Salt Spring and worked on the farm together.

Willis's father, Lewis, stayed behind. A coal seam was discovered on the Nanaimo property, and several people made offers on it, including his neighbour, Ed Hodgson. Lewis wasn't interested, he just wanted to farm. When Lewis was found dead at the bottom of a cliff, foul play was suspected. Ed was taken into custody, though never charged. No long afterwards, he bought the property for 800 dollars. He later sold it to the **entrepreneur**, James Dunsmuir.

WOULD YOU BELIEVE?

Willis's elder sister, Emma, became the first female Black teacher on Vancouver Island. When she was only 18, Emma started teaching in a one-room schoolhouse. She was paid 40 dollars a month. Students who lived far away from school boarded with her, including her sister, Marie. Can you imagine having your sister or brother as your teacher?

My Turn

Have you ever experienced any sort of **discrimination**? How did it make you feel? Not good, right? Viola Desmond, who is pictured on our ten-dollar bill, was a woman who knew a lot about this. Learn her story here at the Canadian Museum for Human Rights: humanrights.ca/story/one-womans-resistance.

CONNECTIONS

Joseph Lewis, also known as Levi Johnston, is believed to have been one of the first Black people to visit what we now call Alberta and Saskatchewan in around 1799. Born in 1772 in New Hampshire, Lewis moved to Montreal in his early 20s.

Nobody knows why he chose to move. We can only guess. Maybe he was a runaway slave, or perhaps he was a free man looking for excitement. By 1792 he'd joined the Hudson's Bay Company as a steersman earning 20 pounds a year. The steersman's job was to sit at the rear of the canoe or boat and control its direction. This took aptitude.

While working near Lac La Biche in northeast Alberta, he married an Indigenous woman. His wife's name is unknown, but they had three children, Margaret, Polly and James. He died at 48 in a confrontation with a Blackfoot.

WHY IS THE RELOADER IMPORTANT IN THIS AREA?

Willis and his family are a key part of Salt Spring Island history. If it weren't for the bravery of the Stark family and other settlers, remote areas like the island would never have been settled. Can you imagine living in a place so dangerous? The reloader is a concrete reminder of the physical dangers Willis and his family lived with every day. It's also a link to the achievements of Black settlers as a whole. By taking a chance on a remote British colony, they kept the area out of the hands of the American **expansionists**. Their creativity and ingenuity played a unique role in the area's economics and character.

U'MISTA CULTURAL CENTRE

CORMORANT CHANNEL

U'mista Cultural Centre

Front St.

Cormorant Island

HADDINGTON PASSAGE

JUST THE FACTS

WHERE IS IT? 1 Front Street, Alert Bay, BC, V0N 1A0; (250) 974-5403
umista.ca or **umistapotlatch.ca**

ARE PHOTOGRAPHS ALLOWED? Visitors can take photos everywhere except the Potlatch Collection.

HOW DID IT START? The U'mista Cultural Centre is located on Cormorant Island/Alert Bay on the 'Namgis First Nation Reserve. The centre was built to house and care for Potlatch regalia that was returned to the U'mista Cultural Society from museums and individual collectors. Potlatches, which are ceremonies that tell Kwakwaka'wakw stories and celebrate important life changes with dancing, singing and gift giving, were illegal from 1885 until 1951. Many families were forced to give up their Potlatch regalia to Indian Agents during this time.

WHERE HAS IT LIVED?
The centre has always been in Alert Bay. There is a sister museum called Nuyumbalees Cultural Centre on Quadra Island, BC.

WHERE DO THE ITEMS COME FROM?
Most of U'mista's collection is repatriated. That means it has been returned from collectors and from museums. Those who lost their treasures never forgot. When Potlatching was legal again in 1951, they began asking for their belongings back. Much of the collection is regalia that was surrendered to an Indian Agent after one illegal Potlatch held on Village Island in 1921. Three tribes gave up their dance gear so their family members wouldn't go to jail.

Regalia have been repatriated from the Canadian Museum of History in Ottawa, the Royal Ontario Museum in Toronto and the Smithsonian Institution's National Museum of the American Indian in the United States. There are many items that are still missing. But the U'mista Cultural Society continues to look for them and will repatriate them when they are found.

HOW HAS IT CHANGED?
Over the years the centre has been given lots of gifts and has also repatriated more pieces from the Potlatch Collection. The collection has increased from just over 350 objects to nearly 1,000 pieces and over 10,000 slides and photographs.

All photos are courtesy
of the Umista Cultural Centre

See the many parts that make up one First Nation's dancer's outfit

REGALIA

The parts of a dancer's **ceremonial** outfit are called "regalia."

Some of the items a dancer might wear are masks; outfits covered with fur, feathers, tree branches; neckbands; anklets; wristlets.

Red cedar bark is used in regalia for dances of the *t'seka* (Winter Ceremonies). These dances are also known as red cedar bark dances.

Sometimes dancers also carry things like feathers, a paddle, a copper or a rattle.

When a dance is performed, it is telling that family's history. Songs are also an important part of the ceremony.

Most often what a dancer wears depends on the family the dancer belongs to and the traditions of his or her community.

The most important dance, the Hamat̓sa, is done by many different families, but the regalia may be different depending on what the family has the right to use.

Families have dances that they have the right to perform. These dances have been handed down through the generations.

JUST THE FACTS

WHAT IS IT? This Bak̲'wa̲s mask is worn by a dancer. The name Bak̲'wa̲s translates to "man of the ground embodiment," or "the wild man of the woods."

WHAT DOES IT LOOK LIKE? As with all Bak̲'wa̲s, his features are very skeleton-like. He has a hooked nose like a beak, pointy ears and a red mouth that looks like he is saying "Oh." Feathers are used for his beard, and his eyes are made from brass disks with holes in the centre. On the top of his head is a knot of feathers and hair, and around the knot curls a two-headed snake.

WHERE DOES IT COME FROM? In 1922 this mask was surrendered to William Halliday, the Indian Agent, and to the police so the owner's family would not go to jail. The mask was repatriated to the centre.

WHO USED IT? This Bak̲'wa̲s mask was owned by K̕wa̲mx'udi (Charlie Walkus), who was 'Na̲mgis and Awik'inuxw First Nations.

BAK'WAS MASK

WOULD YOU BELIEVE?

Not all Bakwas masks are the same. This particular Bakwas mask has snakes on his head. The dancer inside can pull a string and make the snakes stand up. Imagine what that must look like!

My Turn

Why is dance such a wonderful way to tell a story?

Tell Me More

The history of the Kwakwakaʼwakw People is told through dance and song. Beautiful masks and costumes make these stories unforgettable. Bakwas performs in two different ceremonies, the *tʼseka* (or Winter Ceremonies) and the *tłaʼsala* (or Peace Dances). (See http://native-dance.ca/en/cultures/kwakwakawakw/traditional-dances/.)

Bakwas is little, about half the size of a grown man. Because he is shy, when he dances, he covers his face. He comes from the woods and occasionally stops to paw at the ground. Although he lives in the forest, he sometimes goes to out-of-the-way beaches, where he digs for **cockles**, which he loves to eat. A similar creature, Bagwis, comes from the sea and is also a shy lover of cockles.

Masks are used in ceremonial and religious dances around the world. In Africa, for example, there are many different tribes or communities and each of these communities has different masks for different ceremonies. You can see some of these masks online if you search for African dance masks.

⭐ WHY IS THE BAKʼWAS MASK IMPORTANT IN THIS AREA?

Bakwas lives in the country of ghosts. He is also the keeper of drowned souls. They say when someone drowns, they become part of the Bakwas's dance **retinue**.

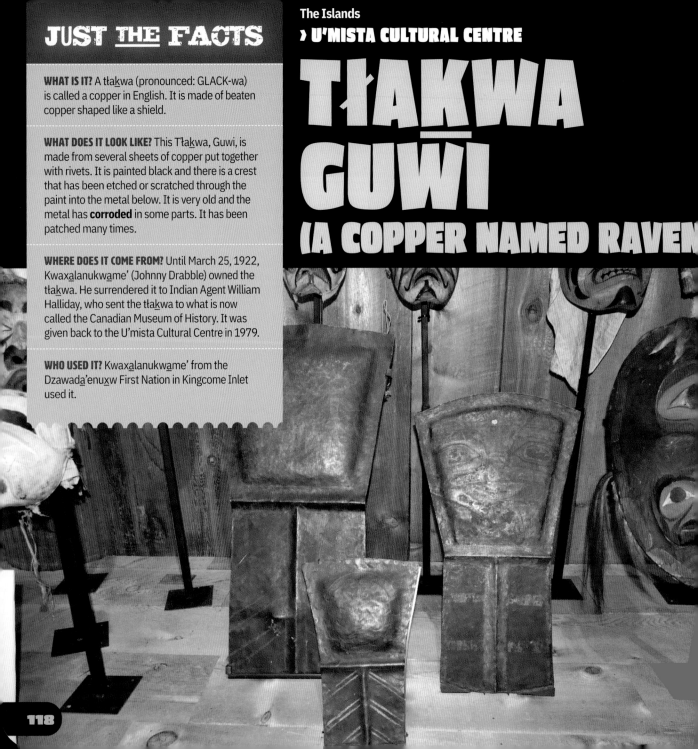

TŁAKWA GUWI
(A COPPER NAMED RAVEN)

JUST THE FACTS

WHAT IS IT? A tłakwa (pronounced: GLACK-wa) is called a copper in English. It is made of beaten copper shaped like a shield.

WHAT DOES IT LOOK LIKE? This Tłakwa, Guwi, is made from several sheets of copper put together with rivets. It is painted black and there is a crest that has been etched or scratched through the paint into the metal below. It is very old and the metal has **corroded** in some parts. It has been patched many times.

WHERE DOES IT COME FROM? Until March 25, 1922, Kwaxalanukwame' (Johnny Drabble) owned the tłakwa. He surrendered it to Indian Agent William Halliday, who sent the tłakwa to what is now called the Canadian Museum of History. It was given back to the U'mista Cultural Centre in 1979.

WHO USED IT? Kwaxalanukwame' from the Dzawada'enuxw First Nation in Kingcome Inlet used it.

Tell Me More

Each copper is like a person, with a name and its own history. Like the Tłakwa Guwi, it can be named for a creature. Animal names refer to the crest of the owners. Other names show how valuable the coppers are. Only Chiefs can own coppers. A Potlatch (which in the Chinook language means "to give") is a ceremony where stories are told and where changes such as births, marriages and deaths are recognized. Guests are given gifts as payment for witnessing the ceremony. Each time a Chief Potlatches, the value of the Potlatch is added to his copper. Every time a copper changes hands, it also increases in value.

My Turn

In museums and cultural centres around the world you will find many objects that are very old. What makes them valuable?

CONNECTIONS

There are many status symbols in modern society like flashy cars, big houses and expensive phones. Even running shoes can be status symbols. But here's the difference between those and the coppers like the ones you can see in the Cultural Centre: These modern status symbols will all eventually wear out or become less valuable. Coppers like those you can see in the Cultural Centre gained value. And they gained value when the owner gave things away!

⭐ WHY IS THE TŁAKWA GUWI IMPORTANT IN THIS AREA?

All tłakwa are important because, for the Kwakwaka'wakw, they are symbols of wealth and power. Like other Potlatch items, they were taken illegally by Indian Agents and police.

JUST THE FACTS

DZUNUḴWA MASK WITH HANDS

WHAT IS IT? This wooden mask and hands represent a female giant of the woods, Dzunuḵwa. These masks are worn by dancers in the tła'sala (Peace Dances) and the t'seka (red cedar bark ceremonies).

WHAT DOES IT LOOK LIKE? Her face and hands are black in colour. But her hollow cheeks and **eye sockets** are painted white. On each palm is a painted face. Her hair and eyebrows are made of a bear pelt. As with the Baḵ'was mask, Dzunuḵwa's mouth is in the shape of an *O*.

WHERE DOES IT COME FROM? The mask and hands were repatriated to the Cultural Centre.

WHO USED IT? This Dzunuḵwa mask was owned by He'wasa. His wife, Mrs. He'wasa, owned the hands. She was from Awa'etłála First Nation (Knight Inlet).

Tell Me More

The Dzunuḵwa is a wild woman of the woods, a member of a family of giants and a terrifying creature. She is said to steal bad children who don't listen or who wander off alone in the forest. On her back she carries a basket into which she puts the children. Then she takes them home to eat them. Luckily, she is not very smart and very clumsy, so the children can often outsmart her.

A dancer's hands are not big enough to show the size of a Dzunuḵwa, so the performer uses the wooden hands to show how big the Dzunuḵwa really is.

WOULD YOU BELIEVE?

The Dzunuḵwa has a family. She is very sleepy and can be easily hypnotized, so the children can escape. She represents wealth to the Kwakwa̱ka'wakw.

My Turn

Many stories we hear as children are meant to teach us a lesson. Compare the stories you heard as a child with those of Dzunuḵwa and Baba Yaga. How did those stories change the way you behaved?

Baba Yaga is a witch-like figure in Russian **folktales**. She's a tall, boney woman with a nose so long that she can lie on her back in her house and her nose will touch the ceiling. She can smell visitors before she sees them. She lives in the forest in a hut that sits on chicken legs! In many stories, she tries to eat children who get lost in the forest. But, as in the Dzunuḵwa stories, the children always escape.

⭐ WHY IS THE DZUNUḴWA IMPORTANT IN THIS AREA?

Dzunuḵwa stories kept children from wandering off into the forest alone, which could be dangerous. These stories often had **morals** for the children to learn. For example, the boy who saves them from the giant might have a cleft palate and has always been teased by all the other children. Now, of course, they see him much differently.

SAAHLINDA NAAY
SAVING THINGS HOUSE
(HAIDA GWAII MUSEUM)

Presented by SGaan Kwahagang on behalf of the Haida Nation

Photo: Courtesy of
Saahlinda Naay
(the Haida Gwaii Museum)

Skidegate

Saahlinda Naay
(Haida Gwaii Museum)

SKIDEGATE INLET

JUST THE FACTS

WHERE IS IT? Haida Heritage Centre at Kay Llnagaay, Second Beach Road, HlGaagilda (Skidegate), Haida Gwaii, BC, V0T 1S1; (250) 559-4643
haidagwaiimuseum.ca

ARE PHOTOGRAPHS ALLOWED? No.

HOW DID IT START? The original museum opened at Kay Llnagaay in 1976. While the museum is where Haida ancestral treasures, settler belongings and items from science and natural history are cared for and displayed, it is much more. You can learn about Haida Gwaii and the origins, Traditional Laws, language and both ancient and modern culture of a Nation who has lived there for tens of thousands of years.

WHERE HAS IT LIVED?

The museum has always lived near HlGaagilda Llnagaay (Skidegate Village) at Kay Llnagaay. In ancient times, Kay Llnagaay was a storytelling town – oral historians would gather there to retell and reaffirm Haida history. Today Kay Llnagaay is still a storytelling town, through the museum!

WHERE DO THE ITEMS COME FROM?

Some items, like the walrus skull you will read about, have been found and donated, and some are kept in trust for families. The masks of the **Supernaturals** were carved especially for the community to present their oral histories and are removed in times of ceremony for dance practices and performances. Many belongings that were taken and stolen away from Haida Gwaii during the Potlatch ban have been repatriated; still, many items remain in other museums and private collections. Two galleries also display an annual schedule of visual arts exhibitions and programs.

HOW HAS IT CHANGED?

The museum expanded threefold with the creation of the Haida Heritage Centre, which opened in 2007. At this time the Elders named the museum Saahlinda Naay, which means Saving Things House in Xaayda Kil (the Haida language). Another important change occurred between 2009 and 2010. Haida Gwaii, the Haida name for the archipelago, was officially reinstated, and the British name (Queen Charlotte Islands) was placed in a bentwood box and respectfully repatriated to the Crown. Guujaaw, former president of the Haida Nation, said, "Haida Gwaii is not only where we are, this is who we are....". SGaan Kwahagang, collections assistant, says, "All of Haida Gwaii is the museum. The building is the glossary."

Learn Haida origin stories
SGUULUU JAAD (FOAM WOMAN)

The Haida of today **descend** from Supernatural Beings who came out of the ocean.

One of these Supernaturals was SGuuluu Jaad, or Foam Woman. She is the common **Ancestress** of most Raven families on Haida Gwaii.

Long ago Haida Gwaii was covered by a great flood. When a reef appeared, SGuuluu Jaad was sitting on it. Other Supernatural Beings tried to climb onto it, but she shot lightning from her eyes to keep them away. Eventually, she let them rest and they decided where each Being would settle. It's from here that Raven families came to be.

SGuuluu Jaad was called "She of the Powerful Face" because of her ability to shoot lightning from her eyes.

This mask was carved by Chief 7IDANsuu (James Hart) in 2010.

SGuuluu Jaad has many breasts. It is said that she nursed Supernatural Beings from which the Raven Clans descended.

When SGuuluu Jaad's first child was born, foam came from its mouth and almost caused another flood!

When SGuuluu Jaad is used in ceremonies, the dancer can make the eyes light up. The mask weighs about 27 kilograms That's about ten two-kilogram bags of sugar. The breastplate weighs another 11 kilograms. Imagine what it's like to dance carrying that weight.

Photo: John Wilson, Saahlinda Naay (the Haida Gwaii Museum)

JUST THE FACTS

WHAT IS IT? This red cedar mask represents K̲alga Jaad, or Ice Woman.

WHAT DOES IT LOOK LIKE? K̲alga Jaad's hair is made from cedar bark. Her eyelids are two different colours – red and green. On her face she wears face paint rights. These are designs her clan has the right to wear. She has a copper **labret** in her lower lip.

WHERE DOES IT COME FROM? Skil K̲aat'lass (Reg Davidson) carved the mask in 2010.

WHO USED IT? The museum exhibits K̲alga Jaad as part of the introduction to Haida culture. She is also used in ceremonial dances at special events.

Tell Me More

Between 40,000 and 15,000 years ago, ice covered most of British Columbia. Scientists believe the glaciers formed later and retreated much earlier from Haida Gwaii than from the mainland. Haida knowledge of their Supernatural origins and geological events that occurred over thousands of years ago on Haida Gwaii has been preserved through the strict training of their oral historians. Their stories have been passed down over generations. Here is a shortened version of their story of the ice age. "Thousands of years ago, icefields made their way through Haida Gwaii home. Because certain areas remained ice-free, some Ancestors remained at home. K̲alga Jaad, who hovered over certain icefields on Haida Gwaii, led others down south, where they lived until the earth began to warm again."

The Islands
> SAAHLINDA NAAY

KALGA JAAD (ICE WOMAN)

Photo: John Wilson, Saahlinda Naay
(the Haida Gwaii Museum)

My Turn

Can you locate where glaciers still exist in British Columbia? How do you think climate change has affected these glaciers?

CONNECTIONS

Just because stories come from an ancient society doesn't mean they are not true. The ancient Greeks wrote about a group of female warriors called the Amazons who lived in what is known today as southern Russia and the Ukraine. Many believe the Greeks just made up the Amazons. But science is telling us a different story. Archeologists **excavating** Scythian kurgans, or ancient burial mounds, found skeletons buried with bows, arrows, spears and horses. They had injuries typical of someone who had been in a battle. At first archeologists assumed the bodies were male. But modern DNA tests proved many of them were women. These women fought, rode horses and were excellent archers, which supports the Greek stories of ancient women warriors.

⭐ WHY IS KALGA JAAD IMPORTANT IN THIS ĀREA?

The stories of Ice Woman link Haida oral histories to science. If ice covered the land 40,000 years ago, then the Haida who were led south to warmer climates were already living on Haida Gwaii. By 18,000 years ago, the glaciers had retreated from the lower parts of Haida Gwaii, and the water level of Hecate Strait (between Haida Gwaii and the mainland) was about 150 metres lower than it is now. That's as many as 85 refrigerators piled on top of each other. There was just a small channel of water between the islands and the mainland. The land was covered by meadows and plains. For a long time Haida narratives were viewed as myth by the outside world. More recently, archeologists have come to understand Haida oral histories do indeed observe and preserve history and are incredibly valuable in assisting scientific understandings.

JUST THE FACTS

KUU KALJUU KAS SKUUJII (FOSSILIZED WALRUS SKULL)

WHAT IS IT? This walrus skull is around 42,000 years old.

WHAT DOES IT LOOK LIKE? The skull is not complete. It includes the tusks and facial bones. There is a large hole where the nose would have been. The skull is fossilized, which means it has been covered with **sediment** that eventually turned it into something like stone.

WHERE DOES IT COME FROM? It was discovered on a beach on Xaaydaga Gwaay.yaay Iinagwaay (Graham Island) in 2017 by Nicole Day, Anishinaabe (Bear Clan), and cultural feature identifier for the Council of the Haida Nation. Before she removed it, she photographed the object, took notes about it and recorded its exact geographic location.

WHO USED IT? The museum uses it to show the connection between modern science and Haida oral histories.

Tell Me More

For the last 2.5 million years here on Earth, there have been times of cold weather and glaciation and times when warmer weather caused the glaciers to recede. During the last cooling period, glaciers covered all of BC. Walruses generally live in the Arctic and sub-Arctic. They like temperatures ranging from – 15° Celsius to around +5° Celsius and spend about two-thirds of their time in the water. They live on ice floes and beaches. The fact that this walrus was found in Haida Gwaii suggests it probably migrated farther south as temperatures became colder and ice covered its normal habitat. Today it's too warm for walruses to live on Haida Gwaii.

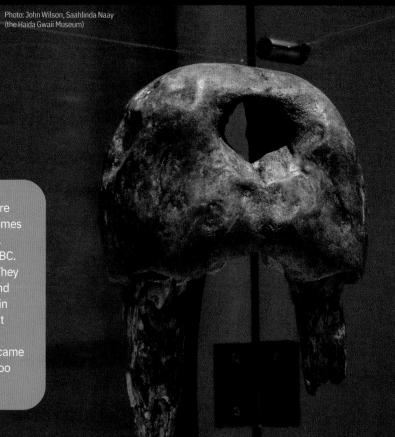

Photo: John Wilson, Saahlinda Naay (the Haida Gwaii Museum)

WOULD YOU BELIEVE?

The museum's loving name for the walrus skull is Wally.

My Turn

Want to know more about fossils? Dinosaur Provincial Park in Alberta has one of the largest deposits of dinosaur bones in the world. Another great museum for fossils is the Cranbrook History Centre. Check it out online (https://www.cranbrookhistorycentre.com).

It's important to know that if you ever find something you think might be important for a museum to know about, leave it where it is. Take pictures. Use your GPS to record where you found it. Be an observer. Write down what it looks like. All that information will help the museum know whether or not the object should be removed. Most items are **documented** and nothing is added to the collection without **consultation** with Elders, Matriarchs and Chiefs. The community decides how the item will be handled.

 ## WHY IS THE WALRUS SKULL IMPORTANT IN THIS AREA?

The walrus you see here lived in the **interglacial period** before the most recent period of glaciation (called the Fraser Glaciation). This is the same time Haida oral histories say that K̲alga Jaad led her people south to warmer climates. Archeologists who work with the Haida Nation are coming to understand that the First Nation's oral histories overlap with modern scientific discoveries. As the Haida share their knowledge, scientists are gaining new understandings about Haida Gwaii's past.

JUST THE FACTS

WHAT IS IT? The mask is of Jiila Kuns or Greatest Mountain.

WHAT DOES IT LOOK LIKE? The carver has depicted Jiila Kuns with a wide mouth, a long nose and wide eyes. Her eyebrows, the area around her eyes, her nose and lips are painted a bright red.

WHERE DOES IT COME FROM? Guud san glans (Robert Davidson) carved the Jiila Kuns mask.

WHO USED IT? The museum uses it to help teach the origin stories and values of the Haida.

The Islands
> SAAHLINDA NAAY

JIILA KUNS (GREATEST MOUNTAIN)

Tell Me More

Creek Women are Supernatural Beings who own the salmon and the trout in the rivers where they live. Every year they call the fish back to their breeding grounds in the streams and rivers of Haida Gwaii. Jiila Kuns is the greatest of all the Creek Women. She is the ancestress of most of the Eagle Clans on the islands. Nang Kilsdlas (Raven) brought Jiila Kuns over from the mainland a short time after Haida Gwaii was created. She had ten children with him, five females and five males. Stories involving Jiila Kuns often teach about respect.

Photo: John Wilson, Saahlinda Naay (the Haida Gwaii Museum)

My Turn

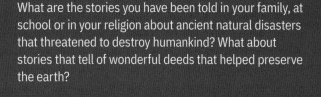

What are the stories you have been told in your family, at school or in your religion about ancient natural disasters that threatened to destroy humankind? What about stories that tell of wonderful deeds that helped preserve the earth?

CONNECTIONS

Stories of natural disasters caused by flood, fires and volcanos are told in many different cultures and religions. They are most often the result of people not following rules set out for them. If you look up the story told by the Māori of New Zealand about Ngatoroirangi, you will learn about how the Taupo Volcanic Zone was created.

WHY IS JIILA KUNS IMPORTANT IN THIS AREA?

Jiila Kuns' great powers go beyond calling the salmon back to the river. She is also known as Volcano Woman. In one story, a young fisherman is wearing a hat with a cormorant crest. When he can't catch any fish, he curses Jiila Kuns and throws the hat in the water. Later that night, he and his friends toss frogs into the fire. In doing all of these things, the young men are breaking an important law – **yahguudang** – to respect all things. These disrespectful acts result in consequence. Jiila Kuns destroys the town of Jiigwah Llnagaay (at Cumshewa Inlet) with a volcanic eruption. The only survivor is a young woman named Property-Makes-A-Noise, who goes on to birth some of the Eagle clans on Haida Gwaii.

JUST THE FACTS

NANG KILSDLAS (ONE WHOSE VOICE IS OBEYED)

WHAT IS IT? This Raven mask is a transformation mask, which means it opens up to become something else.

WHAT DOES IT LOOK LIKE? When closed, the mask looks like a raven holding something in its beak. When the mask opens, in the centre is a human face representing Nang Kilsdlas as a human child.

WHERE DOES IT COME FROM? Chief Gidansda (Guujaaw) carved it.

WHO USED IT? Dancers wear this mask during ceremonies to tell the story of Nang Kilsdlas (Raven), the cultural hero of the northwest coast.

Tell Me More

Nang Kilsdlas, also known as 'Raven,' is a cultural hero who appears in many Coastal First Nation stories, including that of the Haida, Tlingit and Tsimshian. In the Haida world, Raven can present as male or female and can even transform into, or "put on the skin" of, another being. The curious and often mischievous nature of Raven makes for action-packed events that help to form our world, including the creation of Haida Gwaii and North America, and the release of the sun, moon and stars.

Photo: John Wilson, Saahlinda Naay
(the Haida Gwaii Museum)

130

CONNECTIONS

Nang Kilsdlas is a popular character in many Haida stories. He was married to Jiila K̲uns, whom you have read about earlier in this book. Later on in the book, you can also read about Ka Ka Hade, whose figure appears on the back of Nang Kilsdlas as part of the X̲uuya Giixiida (Raven Rattle). Like Nang Kilsdlas, the land otters in the story of Ka Ka Hade could transform to look like people.

My Turn

Think about how a raven moves. If you've never seen one, look up its behaviours. How would you as a dancer recreate a raven's moves in a dance?

⭐ WHY IS NANG KILSDLAS IMPORTANT IN THIS AREA?

Did you know that in the beginning, the world was dark and covered in water? Nang Kilsdlas, commonly known as 'Raven,' is a Supernatural Being that plays an important role in our history. Before there was land, all the Supernatural Beings were floating there, tired. Raven starts to look for land and eventually winds up at the bottom of the ocean. There, an old grandfather brings out two stones and gives instructions on what to do with them. Raven goes back to the surface, blows hard on a shiny white rock, then throws it as far as possible. This becomes North America. By blowing on the black rock, and throwing it closer by, Haida Gwaii is formed.

Without light, no-one can see. Raven flies to the Sky World where a grandfather keeps a box within a box, within a box within a box....the final box holds all the light in the world. Raven tricks the old man into opening this box, then steals the ball of light, flying through the smoke hole of the man's house. Raven used to have white feathers, but the soot in the smoke hole turned these feathers black. Eagle chases Raven, who is flying away, knocking the light to the ground, where it shatters. The largest pieces become the sun and moon, and all the small fragments became the stars.

JUST THE FACTS

ẊUUYA G̱IIXIIDA (RAVEN RATTLE)

WHAT IS IT? The Raven Rattle is part of the regalia used by Chiefs and some SG̱aaga, (Spiritual and Medicinal Practitioners), during ceremonial dances.

WHAT DOES IT LOOK LIKE? On the raven's back is Ka Ka Hade, in the figure of a land otter. He is lying on his back and a **kingfisher** is holding his tongue. On the belly of the rattle is a sparrow hawk and two large eyes representing "Great One of the Sea."

WHERE DOES IT COME FROM? This rattle was carved in around 1850.

WHO USED IT? These rattles were widely used by Chiefs in ceremonial dances during this time and are still used today.

Photo: John Wilson, Saahlinda Naay
(the Haida Gwaii Museum)

WOULD YOU BELIEVE?

The main character on this rattle is Raven, a very powerful figure in Haida culture. When dancers use this rattle, they hold it with the raven's belly up to make sure Raven doesn't fly away.

Betrayal is a common theme in stories around the world. One of Aesop's fables tells of a hunter who had trapped a partridge in his net. The partridge begs for its life. "If you save my life, I will act as a **decoy** and attract other partridges that you can kill and eat." The falconer is furious. "No! I was planning to kill you anyway and now I don't feel as bad about taking your life. You would betray your friends to save yourself." What do you think is the lesson of this story?

Tell Me More

This rattle tells many stories. As a boy, Ka Ka Hade fell into a whirlpool and was rescued by a kingfisher. As a result, he got magical powers. Later in his life he was married to two women, a young and an older one. He loved the young one very much but was tired of the old one. One day the older wife replaced Ka Ka Hade's earring with **sinew** from an otter's tail. When he went out to collect cedar bark, a land otter that had shape-shifted into Ka Ka Hade's younger wife talked him into coming with him.

My Turn

Look up the Greek story of Orpheus the harp player. What similarities can you find between the story of Ka Ka Hade and Orpheus?

WHY IS X̱UUYA GIIX̱IIDA IMPORTANT IN THIS AREA?

BY GIDANSDA (GUUJAAW)

The Raven Rattle is essential regalia of any Chief. The story usually celebrates the means by which a shaman gains his powers.

This is the story of Ka Ka Hade who evaded drowning by being taken to a land otter village. There, he was as a slave to the Chief, until with the help of two land otters he managed to escape on the top of a log. He did not follow the instruction of the otters and ended up snarled up in kelp, cast about in storms and drifting for many days. His people eventually found him near death and revived him with song and prayer. When he recovered, he realized that he gained supernatural powers from his time away.

At the back of the rattle is the kingfisher who is the sound of the rattle. In another story, the kingfisher saves a young boy from a whirlpool. That boy became a great Shaman.

WHAT COULD I DO IN A MUSEUM?

Mike DeRoos   Michi Main

Interview with **Mike deRoos** and **Michi Main**

SKELETON ARTICULATORS, CETACEA CONTRACTING, LTD.

INTERVIEWER: What is the job you do?

MICHI: Primarily, we're marine biologists and, specifically, we are skeleton articulators.

INTERVIEWER: Do each of you do the same things?

MICHI: For me, I'm often responsible for things like finding work, managing our jobs, working directly with our **clients** and collaborating with them on various aspects of the project, like coming up with the story we're trying to tell with each project. We participate together in the design at the **conceptual** stage. Then I'm more of an articulation assistant. I help with various aspects of the physical job, more crafty things like painting and sculpting, gluing bones, that kind of thing.

MIKE: My job is more on the technical side. It's a mix between engineering, welding, **fabrication** and metalwork. And more of the detailed design of the steel **armatures**, overseeing the articulation, how the bones are going together and how they are mounted.

MICHI: Mike is in charge of the more stinky aspects of our job.

INTERVIEWER: What is the stinkiest part of your job?

MICHI: He will do the main work on the collection side. So if a dead whale washes up, I'll help organize it. Sometimes I'll go and assist, but he's always there on the ground working with Fisheries [Department] and with the dead animal. Usually, to clean it, we bring it back to our property and do a composting burial and we both participate in that.

INTERVIEWER: Tell me a little bit about that.

MICHI: Usually when an animal dies, we will meet Fisheries and help them with anything they need to do. The collection of skeletons and animal remains of marine mammals is very **regulated**. At the site, when we're going to collect a skeleton, we're going to cut off as much flesh as we can and try to bring back the bones and whatever tissues remain. And we'll set up a huge composting burial.

MIKE: It's above ground. We start by making a "layer cake," with good drainage at the bottom and with horse manure, wood chips and then a layer of bones and then more horse manure. We build it up – sometimes two layers of bones then a top of horse manure.

MICHI: We use horse manure because it composts quite hot, which helps with the degreasing, which is an issue with marine mammals. We live in a place with lots of horses, but we always advocate that people clean skeletons with what they have on hand.

INTERVIEWER: At this point the bones are not together, are they?

MICHI: We mostly **disarticulate** the bones. We keep small areas of the skeleton together, depending on the size of the animal and the area. Like, usually, we keep flippers intact if we can. It's really handy to have them compost in place, and then we can document how they're actually arranged in relation to each other, spatially. So, after the composting is finished, we dig very carefully in certain areas of the skeleton and take measurements, kind of like an archeologist would.

INTERVIEWER: So you're building your compost up, not digging it into a pit.

MIKE: Yes. We find that they compost much faster, much better, if they're well drained and there's lots of air available to the bacteria and the critters that are in the compost.

INTERVIEWER: How long would something like a whale take to decompose?

MICHI: It really depends on the materials you have and the amount of flesh that's left on the bones. And also the time of year. Typically, an average-size killer whale we'd keep in the compost for about six months and expect it to be mostly clean of soft tissues by then.

INTERVIEWER: How did you get into this?

MIKE: It's a bit of a long story, but, basically, as a kid, I grew up building things. My dad was a builder and I loved working with my hands, solving puzzles and building things. And I had a real fascination for animals. I loved biology. My grandfather was a doctor, so I would find dead squirrels at the side of the road and bring them home and then dissect them with my grandfather. When I was almost finished university, I did a marine mammal course in Bamfield. I put together a sea otter skeleton as my class project because I thought it was really interesting and I got to make something. My professor noticed I was maybe a bit more skilled at that than other students she had in the past and she recommended me for a job at Telegraph Cove [at the Whale Interpretive Centre]. And that's basically how it went.

INTERVIEWER: And then you got involved with the Whale Interpretive Centre?

MIKE: Exactly. My father was a builder, so I grew up building houses and doing renovations and stuff with him. When we first got into the centre – I was there the first year they had funding to hire a couple of student-type people – I had to fix the doors and the walls, put floorboards in, and then I got to play with these piles of bones everywhere. After the first summer they asked if I would put together their 60-foot fin whale. I've never been one to shy away from a challenge, and I always like to keep people happy, so I said, "Of course, I can do that." I realized quite quickly I needed to take welding courses and I started looking around the world at how other people did this. It was not planned. It wasn't something my guidance counsellor directed me toward. It just sort of happened.

INTERVIEWER: How does metalwork fit into the articulation of these marine mammals?

MIKE: They're big animals. Their bones are large and heavy, and in the ocean, when they've got their bodies surrounding their skeleton, they've got all the ligaments, tendons and muscles and everything else that holds everything together. So, when we show their skeletons, all that is gone, and we just have the individual bones. We want to put [the bones] back together in a way that they would be inside the animal but without all that connective tissue that's holding it together. So we use the metal to go through some of the bones and around other bones. The metal does the job of what the connective tissue does in real life.

INTERVIEWER: What's the biggest challenge in your work?

MICHI: The skeletons are complex in shape, and often the skeletons are very, very large. One of the most challenging things is designing and articulating them to fit into our particular space. Every project is totally different. There is no standard method or set way to do this. Every project is unique – interesting but also challenging.

MIKE: They're like giant jigsaw puzzles. I've always loved jigsaw puzzles. One of the most satisfying things is getting two bones, two separate objects, and then fitting them together like they would be inside the animal. All of a sudden, the shapes make sense. You can see how the joints work, where the nerves, the blood vessels and muscles would go. It's like when the puzzle piece clicks in. Hah! That's it.

MICHI: One of the things I absolutely love the most is the story that comes alive as we're working on any animal. Each individual is unique, and often we'll learn a ton about what happened to this animal in its life as we examine it and put it together. It's really a very fun job. Another thing that's really fun is imagining the concept we're going for, deciding what we can do with the skeleton in a particular space given what its audience will be. We try to get maximum engagement from people – find the thing that will spark their imagination as much as we can.

INTERVIEWER: Your job is a perfect mix of science and art.

MIKE: You hit the nail on the head.

MICHI: With our skeleton designs, we're always trying to create something. I feel the metal is a beautiful sculpture on its own without the bones. But the skeleton is over-the-top beautiful. There are a lot of skeletons that have been put together all over the world. They are always a curiosity and so interesting, regardless of how they've been put together. We're trying to use artistic sensibility to say something. The armature actually enhances the beauty of the skeleton, if that makes sense.

MIKE: So right now we have been working on this big humpback whale flipper. We've really done our best to put the steel pipe that holds the flipper up right through the space where a blood vessel would run. It looks natural – like it should be there. I think what might set our whales apart from ones that have been done in the past is we have both spent a fair bit of time out in the field studying living whales and marine mammals. We've gained a real appreciation for how they move and what kind of interesting and cool things they do in life, and when we're planning the design of a skeleton, we try to put ourselves in the body of the animal and decide what kind of story it's telling and what it's doing; try to capture a moment of its actual living life and put that into its bones and do it accurately so it doesn't look strange or weird – bring the skeleton to life that way.

MICHI: And we've both taken apart a lot of dead marine mammals as well, and that's extremely helpful to know how they should go back together.

MIKE: A lot of times it feels what we're doing is scientific illustration rather than completely creative art. We use a lot of photographs and video images of the animal, capture an image, get tracing paper out and draw the bones on as we're planning.

MICHI: And we call on research that's happening and people that we've made connections with over the years who work in the field of study of marine mammals too, so we have good, accurate, up-to-date resources.

INTERVIEWER: What happens if there's a bone missing?

MICHI: It depends a bit on what the part is and why it's missing. But if we want to recreate it, if it's small, we'll often just sculpt it out of a hard clay and then finish it like the rest of the bones. Lately, we've been having some of our bones 3D scanned, so then we have access to potentially having bones 3D printed. We've been working with Camosun College's Technology Access Centre. It's so cool what they can do. For our last couple of big projects, we've done all of our modelling through them and it's opened up a whole new world of engineering for us. If there are missing bones that are larger, in the past we would have sculpted them, which is incredibly labour-intensive and tricky.

MIKE: And it's almost impossible to get a super accurate, detailed replica bone by sculpting.

MICHI: But this 3D modelling technology is amazing. And another thing it allows us to do is if we have a bone from the right side and need one for the left side, we can mirror image it and print the opposite side, something that was challenging before when we were sculpting.

INTERVIEWER: What is the material in a 3D-printed bone?

MIKE: It's an **ABS plastic** that basically goes through a little nozzle like a glue gun. It moves around on a computer-controlled track, back and forth, and builds up layers upon layers and creates the 3D-printed object that way.

INTERVIEWER: What questions do kids always ask you?

MICHI: They're pretty excited about the smelly part of our job. Dead marine animals are like nothing else in the world. We have a very strict **protocol** about how we deal with our belongings and handwashing when we're working with a dead whale.

MIKE: Before you get into the truck, strip off all your outer layers and put them into a garbage bag.

MICHI: We've had the situation where a steering wheel smelled like dead whale for about four months after going to collect one.

Marjorie Greaves

Interview with **Marjorie Greaves**

FILMMAKER AND PODCASTER FOR MUSEUM AT CAMPBELL RIVER

INTERVIEWER: What is your background?

MARJORIE: I started out at BCIT Broadcast Journalism. While I worked in news at BCTV, I saw a little tiny ad in the *Vancouver Sun,* talking about a job with CRTV, which was a community TV station in Campbell River. I thought I would love to come to Campbell River and live in a small community and work in my trade. Part of the **mandate** of CRTV was to make community television with volunteers and to train volunteers how to make TV. It was one of two cooperatives in Canada doing community TV. It was truly grassroots and for the community. The museum was one of the community groups. Its mandate is all about living history, so it's a really good fit for making videos about stories about our community and bringing it alive with video. It was a way of recording history for the museum for its archives and also providing community television for our community.

Interviewer: How did you plan one of these videos?

MARJORIE: I worked closely with the producers Beth Boyce and Ken Blackburn. They had the vision. We would do long interviews with everybody. We might only use three minutes of the interview for the video, but that whole interview – even if it lasted 30 minutes – was stored in the archives for the museum.

INTERVIEWER: How did you tell the stories?

MARJORIE: We would edit the film in such a way that we didn't need a narrator. We would use graphics and the people's voices to tell the story. That seemed to be our style. It was all collaborative.

INTERVIEWER: What are the most exciting parts about making these films?

MARJORIE: For me it was awe-inspiring to hear history unfold first-hand. I would run the camera, but I would get to hear first-hand unedited conversations, which I've always loved about my job. Everything else is edited. To hear the story first-hand from history-makers was amazing.

INTERVIEWER: These films are making history again because they will be kept.

MARJORIE: Yes. The videos will be kept and hopefully in a format that can be viewed later.

INTERVIEWER: Who does the editing?

MARJORIE: I actually worked as the editor – I would press the buttons. But in terms of what went out, that was collaborative.

INTERVIEWER: If kids are interested in doing something like this, what skills would you advise them to develop?

MARJORIE: Anything they are curious about, pursue their curiosities and tell stories about whatever they are curious about.

INTERVIEWER: Should kids start making films on their phones?

MARJORIE: Absolutely. Make films on your phones. Kids are naturally good storytellers and now they have the technology at their fingertips. When I was a reporter, I had to have a big burly cameraman to be with. There was no such thing as a selfie or talking into your phone. It's way easier now to develop your craft. It's not so **elitist**. It's not just for certain people who happen to be educated in a certain way. It's available to anybody who has the technology.

INTERVIEWER: So you are going to do some podcasts?

MARJORIE: We are. We have a title and theme and I'm super excited about it. I'm the site manager at Haig-Brown Heritage House. [Roderick L. Haig-Brown was a writer and environmental conservationist, and a local magistrate. He was well known in Campbell River.]

While I was here for the last year, I read Roderick Haig-Brown's book *Measure of a Year*, which is 12 essays corresponding to each month of the year. It was written in the 1940s. He talks about life at the house, he talks about the birds, the garden, their pet cow Primrose and about raising children. So we're going to do a 12-episode podcast corresponding with each month of the year. And the best part is there's going to be a component where we interview Roderick

Haig-Brown's children, known as "the kids" affectionately. They range from ages 75 to 86, I think. They're going to be involved and we're going to interview members of the community and some other family members – we're not too sure who the 12 people are going to be – but it will be bringing Roderick Haig-Brown back to life in kind of a different way. It's making history relevant.

INTERVIEWER: How are you going to organize it?

MARJORIE: We're just getting started, but the way it's looking today, it's going to be a 30–45-minute interview per month. So whoever is being interviewed will be someone who knew Roderick Haig-Brown or was very much part of the family. They'll read a short passage from *Measure of a Year* and they'll tell us why they chose that passage and the significance of the book and how knowing Roderick Haig-Brown affected their lives. Roderick Haig-Brown told lots of stories and he evoked storytelling, really. He was an ahead-of-his-time kind of thinker.

INTERVIEWER: It's like you're getting a 3D picture of Roderick Haig-Brown.

MARJORIE: Yes, exactly. The children are now older than their dad was when he died. He wrote about them when they were children. I'm so looking forward to hearing their perspective of their dad now that they are older than their dad was. It's going to be so interesting. We'll probably start recording in the next week or two.

SGaan Kwahagang

Interview with **SGaan Kwahagang** (James D. McGuire)

COLLECTIONS ASSISTANT, SAAHLINDA NAAY (HAIDA GWAII MUSEUM)

INTERVIEWER: What is your job?

SGAAN: I work in collections at Haida Gwaii Museum. Museums have collections of many different things – artifacts, modern things and we have art. The collections staff's job is to caretake and organize and talk about our items throughout the day. So my colleague Gid yahk'ii (Sean Young) has been organizing a loan of stone tools to a museum in Germany and **liaising** with them on how to caretake our treasures in their collection. We communicate with other museums around the world that have Haida belongings about how to do better with our things in accordance with our ways.

INTERVIEWER: Did you always want to do that job?

SGAAN: I've had a really interesting array of careers, but the museum, specifically our museum, has always had a place of importance in my heart for sure. Even as I was working on other jobs, if there was a project that needed to be done, I gave priority to the museum always and was able to help out where I could. Eventually, it led to a full-time position in the last year here.

INTERVIEWER: What did you do to train for your job?

SGAAN: In the Haida world it's a little different. Our community will recognize Haida **scholarship** and Haida scholars. I went to school for trades. I did auto collision and welding, carpentry and I've worked in all those different fields. But over my lifetime, I've dedicated a ton of time to learning my culture and learning my people's history, learning colonial history and learning how all those things intertwine. And in our community we choose to recognize people for their scholarship in "Haida-ness." In this museum it's less about the letters behind your name and more about the actual knowledge that you hold. That was recognized and harboured in a lot of our staff. There are people like Gid yahk'ii (Sean Young) and Jisgang (Nika Collison) who have gone through Western **academia** and all of us have gone through Haida academia – sitting with Elders, learning stories, learning songs, learning about the intricacies of Haida art, learning how tools were made and being able to communicate that stuff.

But my trades background, my ability to weld, has led to specialized mount making that people charge in the millions for in the museum world. Having a basic practical knowledge of lighting building and electricity, I was able to help with the **infrastructure**. If early on in your life you can get a good understanding of practical skills, translate them throughout your life and follow your curiosities later, I feel you'll be better off.

INTERVIEWER: What's the best thing about your job?

SGAAN: I like to think about it this way. If you won a million dollars tomorrow, would you still want to work the next day? And I think there are many different jobs I had where a million dollars would be the way out. I love working in this job and in this building so much that, if I won a million dollars tomorrow, I'd come back the next day and work. This job gives me the opportunity to get paid and do what I love and contribute to and communicate my people's culture and history to help build a better future for our people. It's an honour and it's one of the most important things to me. The opportunity to work on and in my culture every single day is great.

INTERVIEWER: What's the hardest thing about your job?

SGAAN: There's nothing hard about working here in the museum. I only work on the **periphery** of repatriation, but my colleague communicates with dozens of museums around the world. Many museums have Haida items, and some of them want to give them back and others want to keep them. Some want to learn how to display our items with respect. We help out where we can.

INTERVIEWER: If a kid wanted to do the type of job you do, what advice would you give them?

SGAAN: If you're a young person interested in any museum, the first thing to do is spend a lot of time in museums, ask a lot of questions, help out wherever you can. Volunteer in the museum and eventually they'll get to know you and help harbour those skills. Also they'll help guide you toward whatever they see fit for your education. In our case here, they ask you to continue learning about your culture and to communicate that.

Moira Dann

Interview with **Moira Dann**

AUTHOR OF *CRAIGDARROCH CASTLE IN 21 TREASURES*, AND CURRENT PRESIDENT OF THE
CRAIGDARROCH CASTLE HISTORICAL MUSEUM SOCIETY BOARD

INTERVIEWER: Tell me about your work at the castle.

MOIRA: I am president of the board at the Craigdarroch Castle Historical Museum Society, and my work at the castle is mostly going to meetings and signing cheques, which sounds really boring when I write it down. But it's not, because what the board of directors and I do allows the museum to do what it does. We approve the acquisition of new artifacts.

We approve the creation of new exhibits, such as a recent exhibit about Elinor Dunsmuir, who was a very skilled and talented musician in a time when it wasn't easy for women to make it in that realm. We even recorded a CD of her music, and used the same piano in the castle that she used. Elinor was a character (she liked to gamble in Monte Carlo!), so it's a fun exhibit (it will be travelling in BC after the pandemic).

We look at ways to improve the experience visitors have when they visit Craigdarroch. And right now (it's very exciting) we are at the start of a two-year project to recreate the kitchen at the castle, thanks to a heritage infrastructure grant from Heritage BC and the province. The kitchen has undergone the greatest amount of change over the years, and spent many years recently as the gift shop! But that's all changing as research and deconstruction (then construction!) continues on that special space.

INTERVIEWER: What do you like best about working there?

MOIRA: What I like best about the work I do at Craigdarroch is discovering all the stories the castle holds. I've been involved for more than seven years, and every time I turn around, I learn something new. It started out as a "bonanza" castle, built by a rich guy,

Robert Dunsmuir, to show off how rich he had become with his mining and shipping businesses. But it went on from there to become a military hospital after the First World War, then it was Victoria College (which is now UVic), then the Victoria school board offices, then the Victoria Conservatory of Music and now the wonderful museum structure that it is. I like being able to imagine other people who lived in the castle in other times, and what their lives were like. It helps me put my own life in perspective.

INTERVIEWER: How did you decide to write a book about the castle?

MOIRA: As I learned more and more about the stories of all the people who have lived in the castle over the years, I saw that the material available to read and learn more wasn't necessarily my cup of tea. I decided to write a book that follows my curiosity and the questions I wonder about when I experience a place like the castle. It isn't necessarily A to B to C, and it goes off on some side trails that are weird, but that's how I investigate and learn: I follow my curiosity. I wrote a book I wanted to read, and it covers all the eras in the castle's history: mansion home for the Dunsmuirs, military hospital, Victoria College, offices for the school board, Victoria music conservatory and now a museum.

INTERVIEWER: What is one thing you learned while writing your book that really surprised you?

MOIRA: Lots of things really surprised me, but the one thing that still has me regularly shaking my head is the lawsuit between Joan Dunsmuir, the original Craigdarroch resident, and her son, James. It made them sworn enemies who didn't speak for years (although he did show up at her funeral after vowing he wouldn't). This was over money the younger of the two Dunsmuir sons, Alex, left to James to care for Alex's wife and her daughter. Joan didn't approve of Alex's wife Josephine because she was a divorcee with a child. Joan thought Alex's estate should have been left to her. James (by then the premier of BC and later Lieutenant-Governor!) kept winning in court, and she kept appealing, keeping the case in court. It was only resolved by her death. I couldn't believe a mother could be so mean-spirited toward her own family and play keep-away just because she could.

INTERVIEWER: When you were a kid, did you like history?

MOIRA: Yes! I loved history when I was a kid. I grew up in a very old part of Quebec, named "Lachine" (China in French) by explorer [Samuel de] Champlain because he was looking for a route to China and thought he'd found it! My father knew so many stories about where we lived and the people who used to live there, and I loved listening to his tales. He would often take me to museums such as the McCord Museum or the Château Ramezay on Saturday afternoons. He collected strange historical artifacts, such as tobacco cutters, and we'd spend afternoons at flea markets and garage sales, seeking out treasures, and he knew lots of stories about "stuff" as well. My parents took our whole family to "the old country" to see extended family when I was a kid, and it turned into a castle tour of Scotland, Ireland and England when we weren't visiting family. That really got me started.

INTERVIEWER: Do you have any advice for kids who want to write about history?

MOIRA: My advice to kids who want to write about history is to think about starting like I did with this book. Find a historical artifact or object that intrigues you and take a deep dive into the story it tells by asking a million questions: What is this? What's it made of? What's it for? Who made it? When? Where did they get the material? What tools were needed to make it? How long did it take to make? Where was it stored? What was it worth? Is something like it still made today, or did the need for it fade away? Did acquiring the raw material to make it have an impact on the environment? The economy? Did the sales/ import/export of this item affect the economy? You get the idea, and I'm sure you can think of a million more questions. Another route into writing about history is to think of something you do today, everyday (like go to school), and then imagine what it might have been like for someone like you (or not like you!) to have done the same thing in 1864, in Charlottetown, PEI. Or New France in 1773. Or Scotland in 1919. You might have to do some research as you go along, but that will only help your imagination. I can only encourage your interest and love for history! You can learn a lot that will not only help you envision solutions in the here and now, but in the future.

TWENTY WAYS YOU CAN USE THIS BOOK

1. Pick an image from one of the two-page spreads and play the game I Spy with your friends or family.

2. Make up an alphabet game.

3. Choose a museum and play a rhyming game. For example, using the Whale Interpretive Centre, "I rhyme with pail. I am a (whale)."

4. Use the glossary to learn new words. Pick a word of the day.

5. Use the boldfaced words in the book to play a word game with your friends or family. Each person looks up the definition of their word and then makes up two more definitions. The others have to guess the correct one.

6. Find the location of a museum or centre on a map. Find out everything you can about the nearest town or city.

7. Pick your favourite item in the book. Think about all the different ways that item could be used.

8. Go to the library or use the computer to do additional research about an item.

9. Many items in the book are described with measurement. To get a better idea of how large or small an item is, try comparing it to a school bus. (The average school bus is 10.66 metres long and 2.5 metres wide). For weight, compare the weight of the item to your own weight, or to the weight of your friends or family.

10. Practise categorizing. How many different categories can one item fit into? How few categories could be used to describe all the items in the book?

11. Pretend you are a reporter. Write down the questions you would like to ask the museum/centre curator about the items you've read about.

12. What's your favourite? Pick your favourite item, picture, word or fact in the book. Why is it your favourite?

13. There are many controversial stories behind the items in museums and centres. Come up with some explanations about why things happen.

14. Find similarities between items in different museums or centres.

15. Visit a museum that isn't in the book. Take your own pictures (if you are allowed), find out the information and try to design a new page for the book.

16. Is there anything we've missed? Create additional subheadings for information you think is missing from the museum pages.

17. Visit a museum in the book and find other items that should have been included.

18. You have read about four jobs associated with museums. What other types of jobs might museums need?

19. Think about what items in the book still exist where you live (town, city, province).

20. Pick an item you own and think about why it belongs in a museum. Make a new page for the book about your item.

AFTERWORD

Now that you've finished our book, tell us, which voices stood out for you? Whose voice do you still hear? Were there voices in this book you'd never heard before? People whose stories gave you fresh ideas about what you thought you knew? Was there someone in this book who inspired you? Made you want to try something new, or become involved in a community cause? Did some stories make you so angry you felt like shouting? Or crying? Or both?

Writing this book, we also felt a wide range of emotions. We heard stories of great kindness, as well as terrible cruelty. There were voices that took our breaths away. Others that made us ashamed of our government and our past.

We learned a lot about the importance of listening and allowing everyone to have a voice. The people we met through writing this book changed us. The stories they told us gave us a more balanced view of the history of our province and country. This is the strength of listening to many voices. It helps to remind us that change is always possible, that we can learn from our history and that we are not alone. There are people from a wide range of cultures all sharing the same goal, just to be heard.

Our hope is from now on, whenever you visit a museum, you will make sure to listen to all the voices that are there and ask about those that are missing.

ACKNOWLEDGEMENTS

The authors gratefully acknowledge the contributions of the following people to this book: Lee Boyko, executive director, Montana Stanley, collections and exhibits manager, Sooke Region Museum and Visitor Centre; Bruce Davies, curator, Moira Dann, president, Craigdarroch Castle; Christeah Dupont, assistant curator, Jeannine Worthing, visitor experience and programming coordinator, Kelly Black, executive director, Point Ellice House Museum and Gardens; Brittany V. Vis, executive director, Jeffrey Olafson, collections coordinator, the Maritime Museum of British Columbia; Lorraine Bayford, programs coordinator/curator of education, Neil Malbon, collections curator, BC Interior Forestry Museum and Forest Discovery Centre; John Fulker, president of the Salt Spring Farmers' Heritage Foundation, Bob Rush, honorary life member of the Salt Spring Historical Society, Salt Spring Museum. A special thank you to Alwynne Ling for the photographs.

Thank you to Shelley Harding, museum coordinator/education curator, Kirsten Smith, collections curator, Alberni Valley Museum, and to Ḥaa'yuups, head of the House of Taḵiishtaḵamlthat-ḥ, of the Huupach'esat-ḥ First Nation for his contribution, but also for his exceptional history lessons. Thank you to Sophie Vanderbanck, senior aquarist, Laura Griffith-Cochrane, curator, at the Ucluelet Aquarium; Netanja Waddell, manager, Jesse Recalma, First Nations consultant, Graham Beard, paleontology consultant, Qualicum Beach Museum; Rosslyn Shipp, executive director, Sasha Hnatiuk, exhibition assistant, Cumberland Museum and Archives. Thank you to Beth Boyce, curator, Megan Purcell, collections manager, Bill Henderson and family, the Matsunaga family, and the Quocksister/Kwawkseestahla family, Marjorie Greaves, filmmaker, Museum at Campbell River; Mary Borrowman, director/treasurer, the Whale Interpretive Centre at Telegraph Cove, Michael deRoos and Michiru Main of Cetacea.

A special thank you to Juanita Johnstone, interim executive director, Kimberly Willie, arts program and collections assistant, U'mista Cultural Centre; and Jisgang (Nika Collison), executive director, SG̱aan Kwahagang (James D. McGuire), collections assistant, Gid yahk'ii (Sean Young), collections manager and archeologist, Saahlinda Naay (Haida Gwaii Museum), for providing their knowledge and sharing their cultures and histories so patiently.

The authors gratefully acknowledge permission to print "Piika-uu (Decorative Basket)," copyright © Ḥaa'yuups, Head of the House of Taḵiishtaḵamlthat-ḥ, of the Huupach'esat-ḥ First Nation, and "Interview with SG̱aan Kwahagang (James D. McGuire), Collections Assistant, Saahlinda Naay (Haida Gwaii Museum)," copyright © SG̱aan Kwahagang (James D. McGuire).

Thank you for going above and beyond. Haawa (thank you) to Haida Gwaii, our Ancestors and the Supernatural Beings. Haawa to the Hereditary Leaders, Matriarchs, Elders, artists, and other scholars of our Nation, that share their knowledge with Saahlinda Naay (the Haida Gwaii Museum) so we can share it too.

GLOSSARY

abandoned: Left alone.

abolitionist: A person who worked to get rid of slavery during the 19th century.

ABS plastic: This type of plastic can be melted at a very high temperature, which makes it an excellent material for 3D printing.

academia: Having to do with formal schooling, like colleges and universities.

aka: Stands for "also known as"; an alternative name.

alchemist: A person who changes something through what appears to be magic.

alevin: Newly hatched salmon still attached to its egg sac.

amateur: Unpaid sports player, not professionally paid.

amnesty: An official pardon.

ancestress: The woman from whom your family tree starts, or a woman very far back on your family tree.

anglicized: A word in another language that is turned into an English word.

aptitude: A natural talent.

archeological investigation: Digging in a place people lived in the past to find out about their culture.

archeologists: People who study human history by digging at places where people have lived.

archipelago: A string of islands.

archival materials: Most often paper items that are important to the history of a place.

armatures: Structures.

articulated: Connected.

assimilated: To become part of the European settlers' culture.

attendants: During a ceremonial dance, the people who assist the dancer.

baptizing: A Christian rite of admitting someone into a specific church. It usually involves water.

barnacles: Crustaceans that have a hard outer shell and live on rocks, boats and even other animals like whales.

bayonet: A dagger at the end of a rifle.

behavioural ecologist: A person who studies plant or animal behaviour.

betrayed: If someone is disloyal to you – like they told everyone a secret you asked them not to tell.

bias: An idea or belief preferred by someone who won't give an equal chance to any other points of view.

bind pigments: Something that holds colour.

blacklisted: Prevented from working anywhere, usually by an organization.

Bronze Age: During this time period, humans started making tools and weapons out of bronze.

cable station: In the early 20th century, a place where messages could be sent and received.

caricature: An image of a person (or animal) with exaggerated features for fun.

cast: An object made using a mold.

Caucasian: White-skinned people, of European origin.

centennial: Celebration of 100 years.

cephalopods: In Greek, meaning "head-foot." They are a type of mollusc with a head and tentacles.

ceremonial: Used at a gathering of people who are celebrating something.

chignon: A type of hairstyle where long hair is coiled into a bun at the neck.

christened: A special dedication ceremony for ships.

clients: Someone who is paying you for a service.

cockles: A type of shellfish.

collection items: Objects that are collected for a museum.

colonial: A period of time when a country is ruled by a more powerful country.

commerce: The act of buying and selling.

commissioned: An order to make or do something for payment.

community cookbook: Recipes collected by a member of a group used to raise money, or as souvenirs.

conceptual: Relating to ideas.

confiscated: Taken away.

consent: Agreeing to.

conservation: To work to protect our natural resources.

consultation: Discussion.

corroded: Become damaged.

crests: Images of Supernatural beings or animals. Crests belong to families and tell their stories, rights and responsibilities.

critical habitat: A place that is necessary for the survival of a species.

culture: The way a group of people live. Their set of beliefs, values, morals and customs.

currency: Money.

debris: Garbage or trash.

decoy: A person or thing used to mislead or lure an animal or person into a trap or danger.

deities: Gods and goddesses.

descend: Come from.

descendants: People who are related to a person or a group of people who were alive in the past.

digitized: Scanned from a hard copy, like a photograph, and put on a computer.

disarticulate: Take apart.

discrimination: Treating someone unfairly mainly because of their race, age, religion, sex or gender.

dismantled: Taken apart.

diverse: Different.

documented: Recorded in writing and photographs.

dorsal fin: The fin found on a whale or dolphin's back.

durable: Made to last.

echolocation: How some animals know where things are. They produce sound waves and wait for the echo. Whales' sound waves go through water.

economic: Facts concerning how money is used.

economy: A place's wealth connected to what is made and sold.

ecosystem: A community of living things that interact with each other and with the environment around them.

eczema: A skin condition that makes the skin red and itchy.

electrodes: Conductors that carry electrical current into an object that isn't metal.

elitist: The idea that only the rich or well-educated may participate in an activity.

enamelware: Cookware that is made of metal, aluminum or cast iron, and coated with powdered glass.

entrepreneur: Someone who takes on a risk to start their own business.

establishing: To set up or start something like a system, rules or a company.

estuaries: The places where rivers meet the sea. Salt and fresh water mix in an estuary.

etiquette: Rules of behaviour for a certain group.

excavating: Recording, preserving and finding things from the past.

excavation site: In archeology this is known as the "dig" being worked on.

expansionists: Followers of the idea that countries can make themselves more powerful through taking over another area or areas.

extremist: A person who has religious or political views they are willing to go to great lengths for.

eye sockets: The holes in the skull where the eyes sit.

fabrication: Putting parts together, creating something.

faller: A person who makes a living cutting down trees.

fantail: A part of a ship at the very back.

fasting: To not eat for a certain amount of time.

Field of Reeds: The ancient Egyptian's version of heaven.

first-order lenses: Lenses that are compacted by separating them into layers.

fleet: A group of ships that sail together.

flourish: To do well.

folktales: Stories passed down from generation to generation.

foundation skids: A base of a building that's portable.

framing: These are the ribs of the ship.

Free Black: Black people who were born during slavery who were not slaves.

freight shed: The place where goods are stored before (or after) they are shipped.

fry: Very young fish.

fur trapper: A person who catches animals for food or fur.

geometric: A collection of shapes like squares, triangles and rectangles.

goods: Objects.

grand tour: A traditional trip through Europe taken by well-off people.

Great Depression: A worldwide financial disaster.

gunny sack: A bag usually made of natural fibres.

gunwhales: The upper edge of the side of a boat.

habitat: The place where an animal lives.

hand loggers: People who cut down trees with hand saws and axes (without machines).

heritage: History and ancestry.

hull: The body of a ship.

icon: A person or thing that is highly respected.

illegal: Not legal, against the law.

illuminated manuscripts: Handwritten books painted and decorated with metals like gold and silver.

impact: Effect.

in trust: An item that belongs to a person, family or group that is held and protected by another person, family or group.

Indian Agents: People who represented the Canadian government on reserves between the 1830s and the 1960s.

inducted: Welcomed into.

infrastructure: The systems that make a building work, like lighting, heating, equipment and technology.

injustices: Unfairness.

inkwells: Small containers filled with ink that are used by someone to write.

inscriptions: Words written on a monument, a book, or something special like a trophy or a piece of jewelry.

interglacial period: A time in Earth's millions of years of history when the earth warms and glaciers melt. We are in an interglacial period right now.

internment camp: A prison camp for people considered to be the enemy.

intertidal: Space between high tides and low tides.

invertebrates: Animals without spines.

Iron Age: The time period following the Bronze Age when humans started making tools and weapons out of iron.

keel: A flat blade on a sailboat's bottom.

kelp: Large seaweed.

keystone predators: Have a big effect on the environment by controlling the population of other species.

kingfisher: A brightly coloured bird with a large head and long sharp beak used when diving for fish.

Kwakwaka'wakw People: A name for a group of First Nations People who share the Kwak'wala language.

labour reforms unions: Groups of people who worked together to fight for safer and fairer conditions in the workplace.

labret: An ornament that is worn in the lip.

lay preacher: A minister of a faith who is not formally trained.

Leechtown miners: Gold miners.

liaising: Talking about, helping out.

lineage: The branches of the family tree leading back to the beginning.

lockjaw: A very serious disease that affects muscles and nerves.

log birling: During a competition, competitors are on a log floating on water, which they spin, trying to make the competition lose balance and fall into the water.

mandate: Instructions or orders given by people who are in power.

mantle: The globe-shaped head of an octopus.

marine nutrients: What marine species need in their food to stay healthy.

mast: The tall pole that holds a large sail on a ship.

matrilines: Relatives are traced through the females.

medicinal: Something that helps with pain or gets rid of pain.

metacarpals: Bones between the finger bones and the wrist bones.

microplastics: Tiny particles of plastic.

milled finials: A decorative feature that sits on the top of a post.

mission: Place where the church (in this case, Anglican) preaches and holds services.

missionaries: People who spread a religion's beliefs in foreign countries.

morals: What is right and wrong.

municipal elections: When people vote for those who work in their local government.

musket: A light gun with a long barrel.

necropsy: Scientific procedure to find out how an animal has died.

needle arts: Needle crafts like sewing, knitting, embroidery and quilting.

nervous system: The system in a living being that includes the brain, spinal cord and all the nerves in the body.

Nobel Peace Prize laureate: A person who is honoured for outstanding achievement in promoting peace.

notches: Dips or grooves that appears on the edge of a fin.

octaves: Eight notes of a scale.

Okunev: A group of people who lived in Siberia during the Bronze Age.

oolichan oil: Oolichan is an oily fish in the smelt family. Its oil is highly prized.

organic material: Material that has come from plants and animals.

paleontology: The study of plants and animals that lived millions of years ago.

palisades: A fence made out of pointed and strong stakes.

papier mâché: Paper pulp used to sculpt with.

peavey log roller: A timed race where two people using a peavey – a hooked stick with a spike at the end – compete to roll a log and strike two stakes with a log.

pelt: Animal skin or fur.

periphery: On the edge.

phalanges: Bones of the fingers or toes.

pitch: A sticky liquid goo that comes from a tree.

political: Something that is about government.

porcelain: A clay used in refined pottery.

Potlatch: In English, "to give." A Potlatch is an Indigenous ceremony celebrating important life events. Guests are given gifts for attending the ceremony.

Potlatch ban: Between 1885 and 1951, the Canadian government ruled that Indigenous People were not allowed to hold Potlatches, ceremonies that mark life-changing events and where gifts are given out to everyone witnessing the Potlatch.

predator: An animal that lives by killing other animals.

prefabricated: A building made in sections for quick assembly.

prejudices: Opinions about someone or something that are made without knowing all the facts.

preserve: Keep in good condition.

primitive: Something in the early stage of development.

protein: A nutrient in food.

protocol: The way things are done; a set of steps.

purpose-built: Something that is built for a particular use.

radiation: A form of energy that is transmitted through waves. Some forms of radiation can be dangerous to humans. Have you ever had a sunburn? That is one form of radiation. Nuclear energy creates a byproduct called nuclear waste, which is also dangerous to humans.

radiocarbon dating: A scientific way to tell how old an object is.

recruited: Asked to join.

reformist: A person who favours fixing something slowly.

region: A part of a country.

regulated: Laws or rules that must be followed.

rehabilitation: An action that fixes something.

religious: Believing deeply in a religion.

reluctantly: Unwillingly.

repatriated: Returned to the rightful owner.

replica: A copy.

resilient: People who recover from difficult times.

resin: A sticky substance that comes from some trees and plants.

retinue: A group of followers.

rites: Serious ceremonies that are customs or practices that mark a change in a person. A good example of this is marriage.

rococo: A fancy style of furniture or architecture.

salmon runs: The time when adult salmon swim back upstream to where they were born.

scandalous: Behaviour believed to be shocking.

scholarship: Learning.

secretions: Discharges from a part of the body like a cell, gland or organ.

sediment: Matter like rocks and minerals and the remains of plants and animals that is broken down over time by weathering and erosion.

segregated: Separated.

segregation: Separating people of different cultures.

shipwright: Someone who fixes and builds boats of all kinds from canoes to naval ships and yachts.

siblings: Two or more children having one or both parents in common.

sinew: A tough piece of tissue like a tendon or ligament.

smolt: A young salmon about 2 years old.

snorkellers: People who swim underwater with a breathing tube that sticks out above the water and allows the swimmer to breathe.

soapstone: A soft rock, easy to carve.

spawn: Eggs that are deposited in lakes or streams by animals such as fish or frogs.

species: A group of similar individuals.

squeeze plays: In baseball, when there is a player on third base, the batter bunts, knowing he or she may be out, but the runner on third base may run for home.

standard bearer: A soldier who carries the group's flag.

status: A person's standing or position in society.

stewarded: To supervise, manage or look after.

Supernaturals: Beings that have special powers.

surrendered: Given up to someone who has control; not given willingly.

Taliban: A very religious Muslim group who took hold of Afghanistan in early 1995.

taxidermy: The art of preserving dead animals for display.

texture: How something feels (smooth, bumpy, hard, soft).

Underground Railroad: A network of secret routes, places and people working to help slaves escape to freedom.

union movement: A group of workers who join together and improve their working conditions.

unique: Unlike any other.

virus: Tiny germs that cause disease.

War Measures Act: A set of laws giving the Canadian government wide-ranging powers during both the world wars. It was used to take away the rights of people living in Canada who were considered a danger to the country's safety.

We Wai Kai fishermen: Fishermen from the We Wai Kai First Nation.

wealthy: Having lots of resources like money or property.

SELECTED SOURCES

THE SOUTH + VICTORIA AND SURROUNDS
SOOKE REGION MUSEUM AND VISITOR CENTRE

Triangle Island Lighthouse

Provan, Alec, and John MacFarlane. "Triangle Island Light." *The Nauticapedia*, 2016. https://www.nauticapedia.ca/Gallery/Light_Triangle.php.

"Sooke Harbour News: Maritime History." http://www.sookeharbour.com/sooke/triangle-island-lighthouse.html.

Cougar

Chamberlain, Andrean. "Victoria Unique for High Number of Cougar Sightings near Downtown Area, Author Says." *Times Colonist*, November 2013. https://www.timescolonist.com/entertainment/books/victoria-unique-for-high-number-of-cougar-sightings-near-downtown-area-author-says-1.682898.

"Cougar Annie Tales' Heads to Duncan Showroom." *Cowichan Valley Citizen*, October 2019. https://www.cowichanvalleycitizen.com/entertainment/cougar-annie-tales-heads-to-duncan-showroom/.

Ho, Sharon. "Cougar Hounds in Demand as Big Cats Sighted." *Sooke News Mirror*, June 2012. https://www.sookenewsmirror.com/news/cougar-hounds-in-demand-as-big-cats-sighted/.

Mark, Joshua J. "Pets in Ancient Egypt." *World History Encyclopedia*, March 2016. https://www.worldhistory.org/article/875/pets-in-ancient-egypt/

McIntyre, Sean. "Cougar Annie's Garden." *Canada's History*, July 2015. https://www.canadashistory.ca/explore/women/cougar-annie-s-garden.

Mitchelle, Wendy. "Metchosin's Past: Big Cat Stories Abound in Metchosin." *Goldstream News Gazette*, December 11, 2014. https://www.goldstreamgazette.com/community/metchosins-past-big-cat-stories-abound-in-metchosin/.

"Sooke History: Mazie and the Cougar." *Sooke News Mirror*, April 2019. https://www.sookenewsmirror.com/community/sooke-history-mazie-and-the-cougar/.

Trophies from All Sooke Day

"The Carnival." *Carnival de Quebec*. https://carnaval.qc.ca/en/the-carnival/about-carnival.

Dagenais, Maxime, and Severine Craig. "Arrowhead Sash," *The Canadian Encyclopedia*, June 27, 2016. https://www.thecanadianencyclopedia.ca/en/article/arrowhead-sash.

CRAIGDARROCH CASTLE

Late 19th-Century Black Forest Mantle Clock

"Frederic Japy." *Famous Watchmakers*. https://www.hautehorlogerie.org/en/watches-and-culture/encyclopaedia/famous-watchmakers/s/frederic-japy/

"The History of Black Forest Carvings." *Antique HQ*, October 10, 2013. https://www.antique-hq.com/the-history-of-black-forest-carvings-1673/.

"Japy History." *Japy Horlogerie*. https://japyhorlogerie.wordpress.com/2018/11/02/japy-history/.

"The Wood Carving Town of Brienz Just Plain Pretty." *Swiss Vistas*. https://www.swissvistas.com/brienz-switzerland.html.

Toy French Bulldog

"French Bulldog." *Dogtime*. https://dogtime.com/dog-breeds/french-bulldog#/slide/1.

"Growler, Papier Mache French Bulldog Pull-Toy (France, 1890s)." *The Brighton Toy and Model Index*. https://www.brightontoymuseum.co.uk/index/Growler,_papier_mache_French_Bulldog_pull-toy_(France,_1890s).

Ressen, Jan. "Remembering the Dogs of the *Titanic*." *American Kennel Club*, April 2020. https://www.akc.org/expert-advice/news/remembering-dogs-titanic/.

Stewart, Elizabeth. "Late 19th Century Toy Dog." *Elizabeth Appraisals*, March 2018. https://elizabethappraisals.com/late-19th-century-toy-dog/.

Stone, Megan. "Dwayne Johnson Hilariously Discovers His French Bulldog Isn't a Great Walking Buddy." *GMA*, April 2020. https://www.goodmorningamerica.com/culture/story/dwayne-johnson-hilariously-discovers-french-bulldog-great-walking-70017960.

Toy Soldier

"200 Years of Tradition." *CBG Mignot*. https://www.cbgmignot.com/nos-ateliers/visites-des-ateliers.

"A Brief History of Toy Soldiers." *The Toy Soldier Company*. https://www.toysoldierco.com/resources/toysoldierhistory.htm.

"Vintage CBG Mignot – Two Centuries of the Finest Collectable Toy Soldiers." *Trains and Toy Soldiers*. https://trainsandtoysoldiers.com/blog/vintage-cbg-mignot-two-centuries-of-the-finest-collectible-toy-soldiers-.

Reproduction of an 1890s Stained Glass Window

"The House." *The Bowhill House*. https://www.bowhillhouse.co.uk/bowhill-house/the-smoking-room-new-for-2016/.

Johnson, Ben. "Introduction of Tobacco to England." *Historic UK*. https://www.historic-uk.com/HistoryUK/HistoryofEngland/Introduction-of-Tobacco-to-England/.

Knapp, Francky. "The Radical History of Women Smoking." *Messy Messy Chic*, August 2020. https://www.messynessychic.com/2020/08/10/the-radical-history-of-women-smoking/.

Leighton, Frederic. *Lord Frederic Leighton Complete Works*. https://pro.trackingtime.co/#/project/1304821.

Silver Earwax Spoon

"Stories from Historic Kenmore and George Washington's Ferry Farm." *Lives & Legacies*, February 2021. https://livesandlegaciesblog.org/2021/02/04/ear-scoops-ear-wax-and-their-uses/.

"The Technique of Illumination in the Middle Ages and in the Renaissance." *Manuscript Illumination*. http://web.ceu.hu/medstud/manual/MMM/frame18.html.

"Versatile Ear Wax." *Early Modern Medicine*, March 2016. https://earlymodernmedicine.com/versatile-ear-wax/.

Hand-Carved Miniature Bed

Cooley, Nicole. "Dollhouses Weren't Invented for Play." *The Atlantic*, July 2016. https://www.theatlantic.com/technology/archive/2016/07/dollhouses-werent-invented-for-play/492581/.

"Magical New 4,500-Year-Old Finds Add to 'Oldest Toy Collection in the World.'" *The Siberian Times*, December 2017. https://siberiantimes.com/science/casestudy/news/magical-new-4500-year-old-finds-add-to-oldest-toy-collection-in-the-world/.

Medrano, Kastalia. "Ancient and Creepy Doll Head Discovered in Prehistoric Child Grave Joins World's Oldest Known Toy Collection." *Newsweek*, December 2017. https://www.newsweek.com/ancient-creepy-doll-head-discovered-prehistoric-child-grave-worlds-oldest-toy-764072.

POINT ELLICE HOUSE MUSEUM AND GARDENS

Albion French Range Stove

"Building the Trans-Canada Railroad." *Port Moody Station Museum*. http://www.vcn.bc.ca/pmmuseum/Programs/Building%20the%20Trans%20Canada%20Railroad.pdf.

Chrisman, Sarah A. "Victorian Food." *This Victorian Life*. http://www.thisvictorianlife.com/victorian-food.html.

"The Hospital for Sick Children (Toronto)." *Wikipedia*. https://en.wikipedia.org/wiki/Hospital_for_Sick_Children_(Toronto).

"Victoria's Victoria." University of Victoria. https://web.uvic.ca/vv/1890.html.

Weiskopf-Ball, Emily. "Cooking the Books." *Érudit*, July 15, 2015. https://www.erudit.org/en/journals/cuizine/2015-v6-n1-cuizine01991/1032258ar/.

Mary Augusta's Painting

"10 Things You Should Know about Emily Carr." *AGGV Magazine*, June 1, 2017. https://emagazine.aggv.ca/10-things-know-emily-carr/.

Baldissera, Lisa. "Emily Carr: Life & Work." *Art Canada Institute*. https://www.aci-iac.ca/art-books/emily-carr/significance-and-critical-issues/.

Sassoni, Enrico. "Prehistoric Paintings in Magura Cave." *Scholarly Community Encyclopedia*. https://encyclopedia.pub/784.

"Watercolor Painting." *New World Encyclopedia*, June 7, 2020. https://www.newworldencyclopedia.org/entry/Watercolor_painting.

Blue and White Chamber Pot

"A History of Public Toilets in Toronto." *BlogTo*, December 16, 2011. https://www.blogto.com/city/2011/12/a_history_of_public_toilets_in_toronto/.

"History of Toilets in Ancient Rome." *Toiletology*. https://toiletology.com/resources/history/history-of-toilets-in-ancient-rome/#:~:text=We%20also%20get%20the%20word,deposited%20it%20in%20the%20sewers.

"How Did the Romans Go to the Toilet?" *BBC*, 2021. https://www.bbc.co.uk/bitesize/clips/z8xtsbk#:~:text=When%20out%20on%20patrol%2C%20Roman,the%20toilet%20wherever%20they%20were.&text=The%20toilets%20had%20their%20own,a%20stick%20to%20clean%20themselves.

Palmer, Daniel. "Victoria's Built History Is All Around Us." *Oak Bay News*, February 19, 2013. https://www.oakbaynews.com/news/victorias-built-history-is-all-around-us/.

Pappas, Stephanie. "The Weird History of Gender-Segregated Bathrooms." *Live Science*. https://www.livescience.com/54692-why-bathrooms-are-gender-segregated.html.

WALKING TOUR OF IMPORTANT VICTORIA MONUMENTS CONNECTED TO BLACK SETTLERS

Historic Dandridge House

"Heritage Register Fernwood." *Victoria Heritage Foundation*. https://victoriaheritagefoundation.ca/HReg/Fernwood/Rudlin1243.html.

Watts, Richard. "Historic Victoria Home Belonged to Pioneering Black Family." *Times Colonist*, February 2014. https://www.timescolonist.com/historic-victoria-home-belonged-to-pioneering-black-family-1.812271.

Fort Victoria Brick Project

BC Black History Awareness Society. "The Fort Victoria Brick Project Commemorates Black Pioneers." *Digital Museums Canada, Community Stories.* https://www.communitystories.ca/v2/bc-black-pioneers_les-pionniers-noirs-de-la-cb/gallery/the-fort-victoria-brick-project-commemorates-black-pioneers/.

"Fort Victoria." *Victoria Harbour History.* https://www.victoriaharbourhistory.com/fort-victoria/#:~:text=The%20Founding%20Fort%20Victoria&text=On%20March%2016%2C%201843%20work,%2C%20digging%2C%20and%20axe%20work.

"History of Slavery in Missouri." Wikipedia. https://en.wikipedia.org/wiki/History_of_slavery_in_Missouri#:~:text=In%201847%2C%20an%20ordinance%20banning,serve%20six%20months%20in%20jail.

"Victoria." *Hudson Bay History Foundation.* https://www.hbcheritage.ca/places/places-other-institutions/victoria.

Fort Victoria Brick Project: Charles and Nancy Alexander, Brick No. 2232

Crescenzi, Nicole. "Black History Month: The Alexander Family Was among the First Black Pioneers in BC." *Victoria News*, February 2019. https://www.vicnews.com/news/black-history-month-the-alexander-family-were-some-of-the-first-black-pioneers-in-b-c/.

Duncan, Caroline. "Women's Institutes Play Prominent Role in Saanich's History." *Saanich News*, May 2016. https://www.saanichnews.com/community/womens-institutes-play-prominent-role-in-saanichs-history/.

"Earliest Pioneers (1858–1899)/Stories." *BC Black History Awareness Society.* https://bcblackhistory.ca/charles-nancy-alexander/#:~:text=On%20July%201%2C%201858%2C%20Charles,of%20Douglas%20and%20Fisgard%20Streets.

"Patriarch and Matriarch of 400+ Descendants: Charles and Nancy Alexander." *Digital Museums Canada.* BC's Black Pioneers: Their Industry and Character Influenced the Vision of Canada. https://www.communitystories.ca/v2/bc-black-pioneers_les-pionniers-noirs-de-la-cb/story/patriarch-and-matriarch-of-400-decendants-charles-and-nancy-alexander/.

"Pioneers 1900–Present/Stories." *BC Black History Awareness Society.* https://bcblackhistory.ca/doug-hudlin/.

Plaque 02 Black Migration

"Earliest Pioneers (1858–1899)/Stories." *BC Black History Awareness Society.* https://bcblackhistory.ca/why-they-came-and-the-pioneer-committee/.

Fulford, Robert. "How Vietnam War Draft Dodgers Became a Lively and Memorable Part of Canadian History." *National Post*, September 2017. https://nationalpost.com/entertainment/books/how-vietnam-war-draft-dodgers-became-a-lively-and-memorable-part-of-canadian-history.

Levinson King, Robin. "A Brief History of Americans Moving to Canada." *Toronto Star*, March 2016. https://www.thestar.com/news/canada/2016/03/09/moving-to-canada-an-american-rite.html.

"New Hope for 800 Black Americans." *Victoria Harbour History.* https://www.victoriaharbourhistory.com/locations/inner-harbour/causeway/1858-black-migration/.

Mifflin Wistar Gibbs Commemorative Plaque

"Douglas Jung." *Chinese Canadian Military Museum Society.* https://www.ccmms.ca/veteran-stories/army/douglas-jung/.

Killian, Crawford. "Mifflin Gibbs." *The Canadian Encyclopedia*, September 2018. https://www.thecanadianencyclopedia.ca/en/article/mifflin-gibbs.

The Douglas Obelisk

Adams, John. "Sir James Douglas: Sinner, Saint or Both?" *Times Colonist*, October 2018. https://www.timescolonist.com/islander/sir-james-douglas-sinner-saint-or-both-1.23470993.

Brown, David W. "7 Fascinating Facts about Obelisks." *Mental Floss*, January 20, 2016. https://www.mentalfloss.com/article/73935/7-fascinating-facts-about-obelisks.

"Earliest Pioneers (1858–1899)/Stories." *BC Black History Awareness Society*. https://bcblackhistory.ca/sir-james-douglas/.

Konstantinovsky, Michelle. "Towering Obelisks Are Everywhere. Here's Why They're So Awe-inspiring." *howstuffworks*, December 15, 2020. https://science.howstuffworks.com/engineering/architecture/obelisk.htm.

Mark, Joshua J. "Egyptian Obelisk." *World History Encyclopedia*, January 22, 2016. https://www.worldhistory.org/Early_Dynastic_Period_In_Egypt/.

Perkins, Martha. "How a Man of Mixed Race Helped Create British Columbia." *Vancouver Is Awesome*, February 2017. https://www.vancouverisawesome.com/courier-archive/community/how-a-man-of-mixed-race-helped-create-british-columbia-3046781.

THE MARITIME MUSEUM OF BRITISH COLUMBIA

Dorothy's Bell

"Christening Bells Project." *CFB Esquimalt Naval & Military Museum*. https://navalandmilitarymuseum.org/archives/projects/christening-bells-project/.

MacFarlane, John. "The Tradition of Naval Baptism as Carried Out at HMCS Cataraqui." *The Nauticapedia*, 2012. https://www.nauticapedia.ca/Articles/Naval_Baptism.php#:~:text=Originating%20in%20the%20.

"The Navy: A Century in Art Naval Traditions and Culture Special Theme." *The Canadian War Museum*. https://www.warmuseum.ca/cwm/exhibitions/navy/galery_themes-e.aspx@section=3-B&id=26.html.

"A Recipe for Hardtack." *The Herreshoff Marine Museum*, April 13, 2020. https://herreshoff.org/2020/04/a-recipe-for-hardtack/.

Watts, Richard. "Old Boat Gets New Love." *Times Colonist*, August 15, 2013. https://www.timescolonist.com/old-boat-gets-new-love-1.590032.

Wonders, Bob, with some help from Peter Edmonds. "Traditions of the Sea – The Names and Times of Sea Watches." *Sail World*, February 8, 2009. https://www.sail-world.com/Australia/Traditions-of-the-sea-the-names-and-times-of-sea-watches/-53720?source=google.

"Yacht: Dorothy." *Classic Yacht Info*. https://classicyachtinfo.com/yachts/dorothy-2/#:~:text=Dorothy%20has%20experienced%2011%20owners,is%20famous%20for%20being%20beautiful.

Wooden Rocking Cradle Resembling a Small Boat

"Archaeologists Find Viking Age Toy Boat in Norway." *Sci News*, March 7, 2017. http://www.sci-news.com/archaeology/viking-age-toy-boat-norway.

"Clinker Construction." *Encyclopaedia Britannica*. https://www.britannica.com/technology/clinker-construction.

Groenveld, Emma. "Viking Ships." *World History Encyclopaedia*, February 2018. https://www.ancient.eu/Viking_Ships/.

Weisburger, Mindy. "1,000-Year-Old Toy Viking Boat Unearthed in Norway." *Live Science*, March 29, 2017. https://www.livescience.com/58456-1000-year-old-toy-viking-boat.html.

THE MIDDLE
ALBERNI VALLEY MUSEUM
Emily Carr Painting of Sproat Lake, BC

Kilgour, David. "Six: Emily Carr." http://www.david-kilgour.com/uneasy/chap06.htm.

Quinn, Susan. "Alberni Museum Gifted with Group of Seven Artwork: Patron Donates Group of Seven Painting, Second Emily Carr Piece." *Alberni Valley News*, February 21, 2017. https://www.albernivalleynews.com/news/alberni-museum-gifted-with-group-of-seven-artwork/.

Trapper Doll

"The John Halfyard Collection at the Alberni Valley Museum." https://www.youtube.com/watch?v=kQ9W9hPIB4w.

Silver Tea Set

Mason, Adrienne. "Rescue of the Coloma." *West Coast Adventures: Shipwrecks, Lighthouses and Rescues along Canada's West Coast*. https://books.google.ca/books?id=pN6X7U4mnCUC&pg=PA98&redir_esc=y#v=twopage&q&f=false.

"One Woman's Resistance: Viola Desmond's Story." *Canadian Museum for Human Rights*. https://humanrights.ca/story/one-womans-resistance.

"A Viola Desmond Primer: Who's the Woman on Today's New Canadian $10 Bill?" *The Globe and Mail*, November 19, 2018. https://www.theglobeandmail.com/canada/article-viola-desmond-10-bill-explainer/.

UCLUELET AQUARIUM
Sea Star

Aquino, Citlalli A., et al. "Evidence That Microorganisms at the Animal-Water Interface Drive Sea Star Wasting Disease." *Frontiers in Microbiology*, January 6, 2021. https://www.frontiersin.org/articles/10.3389/fmicb.2020.610009/full.

QUALICUM BEACH MUSEUM
Jade Adze Blade

Hamilton, Augustus. "The Canoes of the Maori." *TOTA: Connecting People Through Culture*. https://www.tota.world/article/1477/.

Branston Generator Hairdressing Tool

Spivack, Emily. "The History of the Flapper, Part 4: Emboldened by the Bob." *Smithsonian Magazine*. https://www.smithsonianmag.com/arts-culture/the-history-of-the-flapper-part-4-emboldened-by-the-bob-27361862/.

CUMBERLAND MUSEUM AND ARCHIVES
Lydia Catherine (Kay) Finch's Piano

Melvin, Sheila. "Piano Nation: Christian Missionaries Brought the Instrument to China, and China Fell in Love with It." *Slate*, September 11, 2015. https://slate.com/human-interest/2015/09/history-of-the-piano-in-china-jesuit-missionaries-brought-the-clavichord-chinese-musicians-did-the-rest.html.

Union Pin

"On the Line: Stories of BC Workers." *BC Labour Heritage Centre*. https://ontheline.buzzsprout.com/1312528/5287493-ep-1-joe-naylor.

MUSEUM AT CAMPBELL RIVER

The Soyakaze

Hume, Mark. "Japanese Fisherman Preparing to Reunite with His Boat in BC, Four Years after Tsunami." *The Globe and Mail*, July 3, 2015. https://www.theglobeandmail.com/news/british-columbia/klemtu/article25271922/.

Floathouse

Callos, Alexander. "How to Make Cellulose Insulation from Newspaper." *eHow*. https://www.ehow.com/how_7885235_make-cellulose-insulation-newspaper.html.

Dzunuḵwa Feast Dish

Haynes, Suyin. "European Museums Keep Talking about Repatriating Colonial Objects. African Artists and Curators Have Ideas on How to Actually Make It Happen." *Time*, October 20, 2020. https://time.com/5901806/african-artifacts-museums/.

Jacobs, Emma. "Across Europe, Museums Rethink What to Do with Their African Art Collections." *NPR*, August 12, 2019. https://www.npr.org/2019/08/12/750549303/across-europe-museums-rethink-what-to-do-with-their-african-art-collections.

THE NORTH

THE WHALE INTERPRETIVE CENTRE

Northern Resident Killer Whale

"Southern Resident Killer Whale." *World Wildlife Fund*. https://wwf.ca/species/southern-resident-killer-whales/.

T44 Bigg's Killer Whale

van der Zwan, Adam. "BC Ecologist Uses Facial Recognition Software to Track Grizzly Bears." *CBC*, November 10, 2020. https://www.cbc.ca/news/canada/british-columbia/grizzly-bear-facial-recognition-software-1.5797525.

THE ISLANDS

SALT SPRING MUSEUM

Delivery Boat

Bodry, Catherine. Exploring Bangkok's canals. *BBC Travel*, 29th August 2012. https://www.bbc.com/travel/article/20120827-exploring-bangkoks-canals.

Francis, Kristin. Experiencing Thailand's Damnoen Saduak Floating Market. *Souvenir Finder*, 7th August 2020.

"General Overview." *Japanese Canadian History*. https://japanesecanadianhistory.net/historical-overview/general-overview/.

"History." *The Japanese Canadian Community of Salt Spring Island.* https://saltspringjapanesegarden.com/history/.

"Japanese Internment." *CBC.* Le Canada: A People's History/Une histoire populaire. https://www.cbc.ca/history/EPISCONTENTSE1EP14CH3PA3LE.html.

"Salt Spring's Japanese Heritage." *Salt Spring Museum/Community Stories*, July 2019. https://saltspringmuseum.com/meet-the-murikami-family/.

Sunahara, Ann, Mona Oikawa, Eli Yarhi, and Celine Cooper. "Japanese Canadians." *The Canadian Encyclopedia*, January 31, 2011. https://www.thecanadianencyclopedia.ca/en/article/japanese-canadians.

Willis's Reloader

"BC's Black Pioneers Are Part of Our Landscape." *Digital Museums Canada.* BC's Black Pioneers: Their Industry and Character Influenced the Vision of Canada. https://www.communitystories.ca/v2/bc-black-pioneers_les-pionniers-noirs-de-la-cb/story/b-c-s-black-pioneers-are-part-of-our-landscape/.

Bickersteth, Bertrand. "Joseph Lewis." *The Canadian Encyclopedia*, March 19, 2019. https://www.thecanadianencyclopedia.ca/en/article/joseph-lewis.

"The Cougar Hunter and the Mineralogist: Willis and John Stark, Brothers." *Digital Museums Canada.* BC's Black Pioneers: Their Industry and Character Influenced the Vision of Canada. https://www.communitystories.ca/v2/bc-black-pioneers_les-pionniers-noirs-de-la-cb/story/the-cougar-hunter-and-the-mineralogist-willis-and-john-stark-brothers/.

"Earliest Pioneer Stories." *BC Black History Awareness Society.* https://bcblackhistory.ca/emma-stark/.

"Glossary." *Hudson's Bay Company History Foundation.* http://www.hbcheritage.ca/classroom/glossary.

"Mystery Surrounds the Death of Louis Stark." *Digital Museums Canada.* BC's Black Pioneers: Their Industry and Character Influenced the Vision of Canada. https://www.communitystories.ca/v2/bc-black-pioneers_les-pionniers-noirs-de-la-cb/gallery/mystery-surrounds-the-death-of-louis-stark/.

"Salt Spring Island Is My Home: Sylvia Stark." *Digital Museums Canada.* BC's Black Pioneers: Their Industry and Character Influenced the Vision of Canada. https://www.communitystories.ca/v2/bc-black-pioneers_les-pionniers-noirs-de-la-cb/story/salt-spring-island-is-my-home-sylvia-stark/.

Simons, Paula. "Strong and Free: The Adventures of Joseph Lewis, Edmonton's First Black Voyageur." *Edmonton Journal*, February 2017. https://edmontonjournal.com/opinion/columnists/paula-simons-strong-and-free-the-adventures-of-joseph-lewis-edmontons-first-black-voyageur.

U'MISTA CULTURAL CENTRE

Dzunuk̲wa Mask with Hands

"Baba Yaga: The Ancient Origins of the Famous Witch.'" *Monstrum PBS.* https://www.youtube.com/watch?v=aS4VCxMeWQM.

"Of Russian Origin: Baba Yaga." *Russiapedia.* https://russiapedia.rt.com/of-russian-origin/baba-yaga/.

SAAHLINDA NAAY – SAVING THINGS HOUSE (HAIDA GWAII MUSEUM)

Just the Facts

"BC, Haida Nation Restore Name 'Haida Gwaii' to Islands." *Government of BC Archives.* https://archive.news.gov.bc.ca/releases/news_releases_2009-2013/2010PREM0125-000719.htm.

Gid yahk'ii (Sean Young). "To Inspire Understanding and Respect for All That Haida Gwaii Is..." Canadian Commission for UNESCO. IndigenousCulturalHeritageHaidaGwaii.pdf.

Graham, Richard. "Back from Whence It Came." *Haida Nation*. https://www.haidanation.ca/back-from-whence-it-came/.

"Haida Heritage Centre, Ḵaay Llnagaay – British Columbia, Canada." *Canada Explore*. https://www.youtube.com/watch?v=XJWUFvIhtDI.

SGuuluu Jaad (Foam Woman)

Gid yahk'ii (Sean Young). "To Inspire Understanding and Respect for All That Haida Gwaii Is..." Canadian Commission for UNESCO. IndigenousCulturalHeritageHaidaGwaii.pdf.

Kalga Jaad (Ice Woman)

Gid7ahl-Ḵudsllaay Lalaxaaygans (Terri-Lynn Williams-Davidson). *Out of Concealment: Female Supernatural Beings of Haida Gwaii*. Victoria, BC: Heritage House Publishing, 2017.

Gid7ahl-Ḵudsllaay Lalaxaaygans (Terri-Lynn Williams-Davidson) and Sara Florence Davidson. *Magical Beings of Haida Gwaii*. Victoria, BC: Heritage House Publishing, 2019.

"Gwaii Haanas National Park Reserve, National Marine Conservation Area Reserve, and Haida Heritage Site: Underwater Archaeology." *Parks Canada*. https://www.pc.gc.ca/en/pn-np/bc/gwaiihaanas/nature/conservation/culturelles-cultural/archeologie-archaeology/subaquatique-underwater.

Mathewes, Rolf W., Olav B. Lian, John J. Clague, and Matthew J.W. Huntley. "Early Wisconsinan (MIS 4) Glaciation on Haida Gwaii, British Columbia, and Implications for Biological Refugia." *Canadian Journal of Earth Sciences*, October 6, 2015. https://cdnsciencepub.com/doi/full/10.1139/cjes-2015-0041.

Moore, Dene. "Earliest Sign of Human Habitation in Canada May Have Been Found." *CBC*. https://www.cbc.ca/news/technology/earliest-sign-of-human-habitation-in-canada-may-have-been-found-1.2775151.

Worrall, Simon. "Amazon Warriors Did Indeed Fight and Die Like Men." *National Geographic*, October 28, 2014. https://www.nationalgeographic.com/history/article/141029-amazons-scythians-hunger-games-herodotus-ice-princess-tattoo-cannabis.

Kuu kaljuu kas skuujii (Fossilized Walrus Skull)

Harington, C.R. "The Evolution of Arctic Marine Mammals." Wiley. https://esajournals.onlinelibrary.wiley.com/doi/pdf/10.1890/06-0624.1.

Hayden, Tyler. "Walruses: On the Tusk of Greatness." *Natural History Museum*. https://nhm.org/stories/walruses-tusk-greatness.

Mathewes, Rolf W., Olav B. Lian, John J. Clague, and Matthew J.W. Huntley. "Early Wisconsinan (MIS 4) Glaciation on Haida Gwaii, British Columbia, and Implications for Biological Refugia." *Canadian Journal of Earth Sciences*, October 6, 2015. https://cdnsciencepub.com/doi/full/10.1139/cjes-2015-0041.

Pickrell, John. "How Can I Become a Fossil?" *BBC*. https://www.bbc.com/future/article/20180215-how-does-fossilisation-happen.

"Ten Atlantic Walrus Facts." *Oceanwide Expeditions*. https://www.youtube.com/watch?v=NASAFn6AYVo.

"Walrus Habitat and Distribution." *Seaworld Parks and Entertainment*. https://seaworld.org/animals/all-about/walrus/habitat/.

Jiila Kuns (Greatest Mountain)

Contributions to the Ethnology of the Haida, edited by John. R. Swanton, reprinted by the Council of the Haida Nation, 2004.

Gina Suuda Tl'l X̱asii~Came to Tell Something: Art & Artist in Haida Society, edited by Jisgang Nika Collison, Haida Gwaii Museum Press, 2014.

HlG̱aagilda Xaayda Kil Naay Ḵ'aalang (Skidegate Haida Language Glossary), by the Elders of the HlG̱ aagilda Xaayda Kil Naay (Skidegate Haida Immersion Program), 2016.

Nang Kilsdlas (One Whose Voice Is Obeyed)

Contributions to the Ethnology of the Haida, edited by John. R. Swanton, reprinted by the Council of the Haida Nation, 2004.

Gina Suuda Tl'l X̱asii~Came to Tell Something: Art & Artist in Haida Society, edited by Jisgang Nika Collison, Haida Gwaii Museum Press, 2014.

HlG̱aagilda Xaayda Kil Naay Ḵ'aalang (Skidegate Haida Language Glossary), by the Elders of the HlG̱ aagilda Xaayda Kil Naay (Skidegate Haida Immersion Program), 2016.

"Raven: A Haida Creation Story." https://www.youtube.com/watch?v=oxA1W7XiteY.

Reid, Bill, and Robert Bringhurst. "The Raven Steals the Light." In *The Raven Steals the Light*. Vancouver, BC: Douglas & McIntyre, 1984. Canadian Museum of History. https://www. historymuseum.ca/cmc/exhibitions/aborig/reid/reid14e.html.

Skaai of the Qquuna Qiighawaai (John Sky). "Raven Travelling." *CanLit Guides*. https://canlitguides. ca/canlit-guides-editorial-team/orature-and-literature/raven-travelling-by-john-sky-skaai-of-the-qquuna-qiighawaai/.

Xuuya Giixiida (Raven Rattle)

Aesop's Fables. "The Hunter and the Partridge." *HooplaKidz*. https://www.youtube.com/watch?v=ZwfsP55mMqE.

"Ron Hamilton (Nuu-chah-nulth) on Raven Rattles." https://vimeo.com/202399046.

ABOUT THE AUTHORS

S. Lesley Buxton is the author of the award-winning memoir *One Strong Girl: Surviving the Unimaginable – A Mother's Memoir*. Her essays have appeared in *Hazlitt*, *Today's Parent*, *Still Standing*, *This Magazine*, and in the Caitlin Press anthology *Love Me True*. An excerpt of *One Strong Girl* appeared in the March 2019 issue of *Reader's Digest* and has been translated into Spanish. For 18 years, she ran her own business, travelling around Ottawa and western Quebec teaching theatre and creative writing to children and teens. She has an MFA in creative nonfiction from the University of King's College in Halifax, Nova Scotia. To learn more about her, visit slesleybuxton.com.

Sue Harper is a retired secondary school teacher who has a BSc in psychology, an MA in English language and literature and an MFA in creative nonfiction. She has co-authored ten textbooks for the Ontario secondary English curriculum, and has written three books for reluctant readers as part of the series *The Ten*, published by Scholastic. Her writing can also be found in magazines in Canada (*NUVO Magazine*, *Okanagan Life*), the United Kingdom (*France Magazine*) and New Zealand (*North and South Magazine*, *Forest and Bird*). In 2019, she published her memoir, *Winter in the City of Light: A Search for Self in Retirement*. She is the only person she knows who has explored all six hectares of Paris's Louvre Museum. To learn more, visit seniornomad.wordpress.com.

INDEX

RMB | Rocky Mountain Books Ltd.
rmbooks.com
@rmbooks
facebook.com/rmbooks

Cataloguing data available from Library and Archives Canada
ISBN 9781771605069 (softcover)
ISBN 9781771605076 (electronic)

Design: RMB/Friction Creative

Printed and bound in China

We would like to also take this opportunity to acknowledge the traditional territories upon which we live and work. In Calgary, Alberta, we acknowledge the Niitsítapi (Blackfoot) and the people of the Treaty 7 region in Southern Alberta, which includes the Siksika, the Piikuni, the Kainai, the Tsuut'ina, and the Stoney Nakoda First Nations, including Chiniki, Bearpaw, and Wesley First Nations. The City of Calgary is also home to Métis Nation of Alberta, Region III. In Victoria, British Columbia, we acknowledge the traditional territories of the Lkwungen (Esquimalt and Songhees), Malahat, Pacheedaht, Scia'new, T'Sou-ke, and W̱SÁNEĆ (Pauquachin, Tsartlip, Tsawout, Tseycum) peoples.

We acknowledge the financial support of the Government of Canada through the Canada Book Fund and the Canada Council for the Arts, and of the province of British Columbia through the British Columbia Arts Council and the Book Publishing Tax Credit.